THE TRAVELLING MONKEY LION

A catalogue record for this
work is available from the
NATIONAL
LIBRARY   National Library of Australia
OF AUSTRALIA

Steenkamp, Rynhardt (author)
The Travelling Monkey Lion
ISBN 978-1-922803-20-7
Travel

Typeset Whitman 11/16 and Visage Bold 22/26
Cover and book design by Green Hill Publishing

THE TRAVELLING MONKEY LION

AN ABSTRACT ANALOGY WITH TRAVEL STORIES AND TRUTHS THAT WILL INSPIRE YOUR NEXT TRIP

RYNHARDT STEENKAMP

This book is dedicated to my best friend,
wife and travel companion, Danielle.

I love you - always

LIST OF ADVENTURES

INTRODUCTION

I have written this book to encourage people to travel and to explain how travelling can enrich your life and help you to excel in personal growth. It is a travel memoir written to encourage readers around the world to make travelling a priority. The content is based on true stories from my own personal experiences and I hope that they will motivate you to become a member of our travel community, inspiring you to explore the world.

I believe that finding out the essence and truths of who you really are can only be found, or at the very least accelerated, by the wisdom and knowledge discovered through exploring the unknown. I want this book to enable and encourage you to recognise and experience your own travelling adventures. It should be manifested in the urgency to compile itineraries and plan trips that will enable you to discover or rediscover your true self. We are fortunate to live in a world where it is easier to travel than ever before - it is one of the greatest gifts of our time.

The only way in which I could convey the importance of the matter was to share and explore what I have discovered on my own journey. These stories will have certain suggestions, findings and learnings that I hope you will find relatable. Further, I introduce the Monkey Lion analogy in the title of this journey. In short, it refers to the transformational, fun and adventurous outlook of travelling with the mind of a monkey and the heart of a lion.

This concept borrowed from the animal kingdom has depth that requires some explanation. I believe that in order to discover and explore the world, you need to take control of your fearful and negative thoughts, which have served you much as an insect deterrent when you meet the famous travel bug. I refer to the indoctrinated thoughts that will give you reasons for not using the opportunity to travel the world. Society would suggest that consumerism and materialism are the essence of happiness. That is nonsense, and if you are reading this book, you probably already have a suspicion that they do not provide sustainable contentment or happiness. When I refer to monkey brain thinking, I want you to imagine all the negative and naïve thoughts that made you believe you couldn't do it, and eliminate them immediately.

The second part of the Monkey Lion analogy consists of the other ingredient essential to exploring the world: the importance of taking action and being brave. Once you have transformed your mind to thinking positively about travelling, you can start making plans - or even buy a plane ticket. However, in order to take action, you will have to be courageous. It is going to require some heart, which I will refer to as your lion heart. It is the part of you that is convinced there is more to life than just being in one place all the time. It refers to the spirit that yearns for adventure, moving and taking risks. The lion heart is what causes you to take action, the vehicle that encourages you to finally move.

A Monkey Lion Traveller is a person who makes a committed decision to travel the world. That person knows no fear, enjoys being impulsive, realises that life is short, avoids boredom at all cost, knows they have more to learn, finds purpose whilst on the road, and constantly seeks the truths that can only be unlocked by leaving the spheres of their comfort zones.

I want to share with you, my fellow traveller, a few of my own travelling stories! They are highlights and lowlights that involve a young man who lived the Travelling Monkey Lion analogy without even knowing it. It is a combination of craziness, fun, faith, sadness, joy, determination, luck and abundant blessing. They are all incredibly close to my heart, and it is a privilege to share them with you.

In summary, this book is for all adventurers, to remind them that it is never too late to dream. God created this beautiful planet not for us to view from a safe distance, but to experience hands-on, so we meet people, see places and make memories.

Remember that you are the writer of your own stories. I hope you will also share your adventures with our community.

The good news is that your journey has already begun. It began when you picked up this book. If travelling has already been part of your life, may this book remind you of the reasons behind it. This is not another travel book that talks about historical museums and the sights and sounds of famous landmarks. This book is about the deep truths that travelling reveals. It is about the characters we meet and the unknown places we discover. It is about the hardships and the ecstasies that come with risking it all to gain what no one else can take away from you.

CHAPTER 1

SANCTIONS AND STEREOTYPES

I was born and bred in the beautiful continent of Africa. More specifically, I used to call South Africa my home. My home language is Afrikaans and I grew up in a very Afrikaans-oriented city called Pretoria. The city is close to South Africa's economic hub, Johannesburg, which is also known as the City of Gold. I grew up in a suburban environment where very few people were into travelling. Our country went through decades of international isolation due to the political regime of Apartheid, which also played a massive role in the lack of interest around travelling.

This changed in 1994 when South Africa became a democratic country. I was seven years old at the time. During this era of political change there were several rumours of an imminent civil war. Many South Africans were concerned, governed by a subculture of fearing change. But the new era in South Africa was to serve as a lifeline to many people who were interested in travelling abroad. The country had reconciled with the rest of the world and we would again be welcomed without any looming sanctions.

South Africa is a country blessed with wonderful diversity. This really resonated with me, despite our past troubles, and is probably the main thing that I love about South Africa. The diversity is a combination of ethnic Africans, Indians, a mixed-race population, and Europeans who migrated during the 16th century. When I was a young man this convinced me that travelling might just be an integral part of my DNA. The fact that my ancestors decided to leave Europe and take a ship to Africa was enough evidence to push the agenda of an adventurous spirit. They must have felt that it was time for an adventure, or more likely, they might have been forced aboard as labourers.

Now, this is Monkey Lion kind of stuff. The heart of a lion says let's go to Africa to work the land (ironically, lions also live there), and the fearful brain of a monkey says that nothing can be worse than the cold European winters, so let's go to a place with no food or infrastructure plus dangerous wild animals (and again, it's a place with actual monkeys). What an adventure that must have been for those people and their families, moving halfway across the world, into the unknown lands of wild Africa.

***

I believe that this same blood also runs in your veins. I believe we were all born adventurers or travellers, or Monkey Lions, or whatever you want to call it. This makes it hard to understand why so many people fear and resist both change and different cultures. It goes to show how we can undermine our true selves in order to conform. Please ensure that such negative thoughts are not part of your thinking, and that you are breaking away from any stereotypes associated with wherever you might find yourself in the world. This is the first step to exploring the unknown.

I was fortunate in the sense that I grew up in a family environment where we were allowed to explore life. My parents granted us all the freedom in the world, but we had to carry the consequences of our actions. I always enjoyed exploring and meeting new people. We all have a unique story that will lead us to travelling, or may have already done so. This is how God designed us - with a special plan that only He can help us find the answers to.

A significant moment in my life came when I watched the scene at the end of the third part of the *Lord of the Rings*, where Frodo rows his boat to a far-off land. I was crying, one paddle stroke at a time. He felt that he had experienced too many things to simply return to his home and could no longer live a conservative or stereotypical life associated with the safety of the Shire. He wanted more and went for it. He could never go back to the way he was. It is exactly the same for all of us once we start to explore and discover the unknown. We experience things that change us and make us different. This transformation makes it impossible to return to what we used to perceive as normal. It is what travelling the world gives you: precious personal growth while allowing your development as a human being to excel. It crafts your character and expands your perspectives.

Once I finished school, I simply knew that I wanted to explore more, see more, feel more, and most importantly meet more people. I didn't have the easiest of childhoods. My parents went through a divorce when I was a young boy and I was left to be the man of the house for my mum and little sister. We weren't financially stable and I remember having to cancel a date with a girl I really liked because my mum didn't have enough money for me to buy a movie ticket. All of this led to rebellion, which definitely encouraged the urge to get away and have a fresh start somewhere else. This almost forced my travelling ambitions to kick off.

You do not have to be nearly as dramatic. Hopefully it started when you picked up this book. Reflecting on my dodgy childhood, I realise that this is probably where the lion heart was born, while to be fair, the monkey brain was kind of always there. Everything in life happens for a reason. I know that is a cliché, but it is true. Had it not been for the struggles, I would probably not have been brave enough to take the risks and bold steps that led to so many adventures. Today I am grateful beyond words that I did, and I encourage you to do the same.

All of my friends had different dreams when they left school. They had dreams involving careers, raising a family, buying their first car, studying at a prestigious university, or simply working hard enough to make a living and become independent. These are all valid, noble and admirable ambitions. However, mine was somewhat different.

All I wanted to do was to travel and see the world. I had one dream, which was to see all seven continents God created. My dream was to stand on each of them with my own two feet, to see them with my own two eyes and to embrace them with my own two hands. This dream is still very much alive today and I look forward to many more adventures similar to the ones I will be sharing with you in this book. It was clear that the world was waiting - and I was ready to get going. I had one dream and seven continents. I was ready to break free from all the sanctions and stereotypes.

CHAPTER 2

WHEN DREAMS BECOME REALITY

My dreams started to become a reality as soon as I left school. Despite my sanctioned and stereotypical background, I had managed to make up my own mind on what I wanted to do and where I wanted to travel. I took the first viable opportunity that came my way and finally got to venture into the unknown.

It was 2005 and I had just finished my final year of secondary school. I could smell the freedom as the hot summer months facilitated the countdown to the end of a massive chapter in my life. At the time it was very popular for young people my age to take a gap year and work abroad. I knew that this was what I wanted to do, and worked multiple odd jobs in order to save enough money to survive the first couple of months abroad.

I was on my way to London, the capital of England and a city that many young South Africans chose as their gap year destination at that time. The first step towards the adventure was to obtain a working holiday visa, which would allow me to stay and work there for up to two years. Receiving that visa was one of the greatest feelings I had ever experienced. I felt excited, nervous, courageous and overwhelmed with joy! Just imagining the prospect of going abroad for the first time was a dream come true.

There were a lot of travel agencies available to assist with the process; however, I ended up planning everything myself while my mum blessed me with a ticket to London - definitely much better than a movie ticket! I had a couple of farewell gatherings in my hometown, which led to numerous philosophical discussions around the first of the seven continents on which to kick-start my one dream, a dream which was about to become a reality.

Unfortunately, two of my close friends decided to stay home as they were both in serious relationships. I remember being disappointed and a bit saddened about their absence, as it made the entire ordeal all the more daunting. Luckily for me, the shining light of optimism and comfort came in the form of my older sister, who had departed for London a few months earlier. She was also the one who sat next to me at the embassy before I entered the interview room for my visa application. No matter how strong we think we might be, we all need a little help at some stage. In my life, my older sister came through for me on many occasions. I hope that you have someone like that in your life, and if not, keep praying. I have learned that God sends the right people at exactly the right time.

After an emotional goodbye at the Johannesburg International Airport, I got onto my British Airways flight and basically danced my way to the seat. Spirit fingers, Shakira hips and all that. I met two older gentlemen from Germany with whom I quickly became friends, and I remember bragging to them about how I was going to take on the world. They laughed as they sipped on their whiskies - politely enough not to crush my high spirits.

My warm and fuzzy enthusiasm was tempered by the harsh reality of the cold weather when I arrived in Heathrow. No amount of whiskey could numb out that breeze. I continued on to my first underground train ride once I met up with my sister. The smell of fresh coffee and freshly baked bread was intense and overwhelming. I could feel the compelling effects of a first-time encounter with adventure like never before. Nothing was scripted and there was no safety net of guarantees. It was amazing that everyone was going about their daily business with no idea of the unfolding moment. My dreams were a reality.

The underground trains and overall infrastructure in London work like a well-oiled machine. Trains are consistently on time, reliable and safe. It's worlds apart from how things work in Africa. The sudden change of everyday life in a First World country hits you instantly, and I recall feeling a sense of comfort regardless of the fact that I was in the unknown. London is busy and things happen at a rapid pace.

People seemed a bit antisocial at first, which aligned well with the cold weather.

Still tasting the whiskey on my lips, I suddenly missed my new German friends. I had one last look at Heathrow Airport as the announcer asked us to mind the gap between the train and the platform.

London presented a different environment from what I had anticipated. It brought about a sense of the cosmopolitan, which I had only seen on television before this adventure. The city is a hub with no discriminating restrictions as it manifests the hopes and dreams of many people looking for a better life. You immediately search for familiarity, only to find that there is none. Was this the dream I had envisioned, or an abrupt nightmare? This was about breaking my comfort zone. This was about making my dreams become a reality.

***

The next month was all about job hunting, which can be surprisingly difficult and scary. I had no formal qualifications and very little work experience. I remember visiting job vacancy offices where they had jobs listed on their system. It became a daily routine of throwing on my only jacket and walking to the hub of potential employment. It was daunting but also exhilarating as I ventured through the streets of this beautiful and vibrant city. You can feel the energy. It never sleeps.

It felt as if I had it all figured out. I was going to get an excellent job, earn British pounds, stay in a house full of

Brazilian women, and not speak to one South African for an entire year. Fortunately, God knew better and I ended up staying in a house with other South African men, and worked as an underpaid barman and later as a security guard doing sixteen-hour shifts. I also ended up partying at a local pub called Zulu's. The pub, named after a native African tribe, became my watering hole for an entire year.

Looking back now, I can clearly see God's hand in all of this. He knew what I was ready for and what I was capable of handling. I had some serious growing up to do and despite thinking I had it all figured out, the truth was, I was oblivious to the plans and the purposes of the gap year I had been blessed with. God shaped the year in such a way that I made friends for life, and because these friends were all South Africans, we were able to pick up where we left off upon our return home. God also placed me in a specific industry for a reason. At eighteen years old, I worked as a security guard in London, only to be appointed as a communications manager for a large security firm in South Africa ten years later.

Being in London made me feel as if the world was waiting to be discovered. I had taken the first bold step to realising my dream. Small victories were what made that initial adventure so special - the first weekly salary payment, the rent you paid yourself, the bus ticket that you bought with your own money, and so on. All those grown-up things seemed so much fun; they were stressful, but I felt free. I didn't have to ask anyone for anything. I was living an independent life and knew like never before that God was my true source of strength. The reality confirmed that it was in fact a dream, not a fairy tale.

I was entrenched amongst people and experiences that would carry me through the challenges I had yet to face. London formed the foundation of my adulthood and served as valuable preparation for my journey. I can only smile as I look back on a year that took me from a boy to a man in a very short space of time.

God used this travelling experience to prepare me for my future. I firmly believe that was only achievable by purpose-fully venturing out of my comfort zone, rowing my boat on the waves of God's grace and mercy. One stroke at a time, just like Frodo. I challenge you to do the same, to stretch your boundaries and allow for Him to intervene and take control. Draw up a list of all the destinations you want to experience and pray about it. Make your dreams become a reality.

CHAPTER 3

THE SIMPLICITY OF SAFARIS, MONUMENTS AND SPEEDBOATS

Discovering the beauty of simplicity through safaris, monuments and speedboats gave me insight into life in a unique and profound way. It disseminated the illusions of a busy society and took me to the source of happiness by valuing the simple things in life.

It was 2010 and I was in South Luanga, Zambia. I was on a night safari with a friend I had met in London - and his parents. We obviously weren't that independent after all. We were watching closely and cautiously as a leopard slowly crept towards a puku antelope grazing in the thick bushes. Deep in the heart of the South-West African vegetation, the puku is uniquely camouflaged; however, this time he was spotted and targeted by this mythical predator. Everyone was dead quiet and you could smell the tension in the fog-filled African canvas hovering over the switched-off safari vehicles. A total of approximately fifty-plus safari enthusiasts were captivated as one of Africa's most sought-after performances was about to unfold. Unfortunately, my friend and I were not cooperating, and we broke the silence a few times as we reached for the ice cubes in the cooler bag between us. Keeping our drinks cold while the puku stared death in the face was not very sensitive, yet heroic.

There was simply too much commotion (not only on our account) and the antelope spotted the leopard and ran off. You could sense mixed motions of disappointment and relief as the puku galloped away unharmed. The safari continued and we kept floating at the back of the vehicle like a couple of Greenpeace sailors riding along the waves of flexible vehicle suspension, saving the puku and liberating the antelopes with our ice cube strategy. We were protesting on behalf of the victims of a robust African food chain. Who would have thought that we would end up being the activists? Most of the passengers did not share our sentiment and could not comprehend our joyous spirits. The liberation in combination with the over-intake of beverages quickly made the situation a one-sided affair – two, if you count the puku. We went from activists to rebellion, silent outcasts exiled to the naughty backseat of the safari vehicle.

Zambia spoiled us on a few occasions, where we bore witness to the well-documented African sunset. The natural phenomenon gives you a feeling of complete contentment. We were fortunate to experience the bright orange and red sky paintings almost every evening. There is nothing like a sun setting over the African rivers, mountains, oceans, and especially the Bushveld region. It truly makes you realise that beauty lies in simplicity. Enjoying the little things is something the locals have mastered.

I remember the famous actor Will Smith saying in an interview that Africa is like God's home, and He only goes to visit the other continents. I promise you, once you have seen an African sunset you will understand that comment. It is one of the most accurate descriptions of this continent that I have ever heard. Again, the beauty of it lies in its simplicity. On this particular trip we did a month-long tour, travelling through Botswana, Zambia and Mozambique.

It was a magical adventure that I had demanded to be a part of a few months earlier. I left behind Danielle (my girlfriend at the time) to go with my friend, but wrote to her daily. I kept a diary, addressed to her, on what we were doing and what we were experiencing. The idea was to give it to her once we got back home; I was hoping to somehow romanticise the masculine safari adventure. God taught me so much on that trip. I see now that it was necessary for me to go about it alone. Remember that it really is okay if you need to take a trip on your own. If you've been waiting for permission, you've got it: this book is giving it to you today. The trip actually brought Danielle and me closer to each other in a weird way, and I assure you that it will most likely be the same in your case. Absence makes the heart grow fonder indeed. It is simple.

One afternoon, my friend and I enjoyed another one of those special African sunsets so much that we lost track of time. We realised that we were quite far away from camp and still had to return to the tents before it got completely dark. If there is one basic rule in Africa, it is not to drive or walk at night. It is simply too dangerous, because at night you can't see the animals and they can't see you. This leads to unexpected encounters with frightening results, as the night sky lacks the light you need to keep your distance. Specifically, hippos who wander on land at night can be a huge problem - and there were plenty of them in Zambia. You also need to look out for predators such as leopards, who mainly hunt at night. Not only did we have to consider these typically active night-time animals, but in this scenario, there were also elephants in the area and if you got between them and their calves you could be in serious trouble.

We trod carefully as we needed to move at a reasonable, yet steady pace. I tend to laugh when I get nervous and was giggling along like a teenage girl as we manoeuvred through the riverbank trees. We managed to elude the animals, but stumbled upon a ranger's cabin. We spent about an hour with him, listening to stories and taking notes about the pitfalls one should avoid while on safari. We eventually felt comfortable enough to return to base camp, after he gave us the thumbs-up to continue.

I remember meeting the ranger and thinking how awesome it must be to stay on the river banks of South Luanga, Zambia. He had a porch just like in the movies and looked a bit like an African Chuck Norris. He was content with the basic simplicity that governed his cabin and the surrounding environment. Who wouldn't be with a view like that? A sunset over the river bank with the shadows of the African wildlife falling slightly to the right. He would dust off his shoes from a hard day's labour and sit back with a gentle-man-like satisfaction, soaking up life in his own way. It was so simple and yet so enticing - a dream for those with a Lion Heart longing for long days in the African sun, psychologically being nurtured by the vast nature you find there.

There is another side to this story. Despite its beauty, rural Africa is a place that really makes you appreciate what you have. Not everyone lives like the African Chuck Norris. I encourage you, especially if you find yourself in a first world country, to visit the African continent, mainly for its beauty but also for its perspective. Poverty is an epidemic that can clearly be seen in Zambia. There are miles upon miles of villages with no electricity and no running water. It makes you realise how fortunate we are to be able to take a warm shower before we go to bed, watch television, or prepare a meal from a wide variety of choices. We take safety for granted. We are privileged in the sense that we can lock our doors or have a means to contact local authorities. We don't appreciate our space or our privacy as much as we should: these are all non-existent factors in the lives of millions of rural African citizens.

There is an interesting contradiction between the physical poverty-stricken areas and the richness of the simplicity I found while on safari. I found it so beautiful and felt unexpectedly envious of this simplistic way of life. The Zambian locals living in these conditions didn't have the so-called worldly luxuries, yet they seemed to have abundantly more in a spiritual way. The simplicity of their lifestyle is fascinating and to a certain extent desirable. Their way of life involves quality time with family and the peace that only an evening fire under a blanket of stars can offer. Not to mention the hearty food they prepare with no diet fads or constraints to dilute their gratification. It is that simple.

There are also no iPads or mobile phones to distract them from engaging with each other. I saw that they still talk to each other and look at each other. You can hear them laughing and feel their delight dancing through the African skies. They find comfort and satisfaction in their meals and family, and yet they literally have nothing of material value. They are a people without balance sheets, profit lines or the ever-lurking shadow of debt. If some of these points have somehow pressed your buttons, then make a note to keep your next adventure simple. Turn off the digital devices that clutter your mind. Make a fire or go camping. Even better, make some plans to take a safari. I recommend keeping it simple if you can.

***

The year was 2006 and I was on a Western European tour with an agency called Budget Expeditions. No surprises there, for a nineteen-year-old London-based security officer who had no choice but to work with a tight budget. Our first stop on tour was in Paris, France. The City of Lights. The tour included a six-country itinerary fitted into a short time frame of only two weeks. There was no doubt that we were doing this on a budget. The means of travel was a bus which seated approximately thirty Monkey Lion Travellers from all over the world. The plan was to arrive in Paris after riding our bus on the ferry that crossed over from Dover beach. We had no idea that this was possible, as most buses in Africa struggle to stay on the road, never mind on the water.

After sailing across the waters of Europe while gulping down on our first beer, we arrived safely in France. We reached camp and after a display of how to put up our two-man tightly fitted lovebird tents, we managed to shake off the feeling of how cheap we were by venturing into the magical city. As evening dawned, we made our way up a staircase that I was convinced would lead to the gates of heaven, purely because of its reluctance to stop and the surrounding atmosphere of intricacy. It led to the iconic Sacre Coeur Basilica. At the top of the climb, I discovered hundreds of young people sitting on the monument's steps. My out-of-shape physique was not impressing any of the ladies on tour or on the steps. I was frantically trying to catch my breath. Imagine one of the Teletubbies swearing in a language that sounded Dutch, cheeks turning more and more red the closer I got to the top.

Standing in front of this breathtakingly beautiful monument, we were spoiled with an incredible view of Paris. A few gentlemen were busy serenading all of us on their guitars, or metaphorical harps. This made me feel better. What really stuck with me was the unexpectedly free-spirited atmosphere in contrast with the busy city down below. There were no electronics to distract from the experience. It was simple. Only a few guitars, a spectacular atmosphere and a Teletubby. I was falling in love with Paris.

It became my sacred monument of simplicity. People were choosing to physically and metaphorically leave the busyness below, and reset themselves with the simplicity found at this spectacular place overshadowing the noise.

The next day the tour operator gave all of us an opportunity to wonder the streets of Paris. I was on tour with five South African friends and it didn't take us long to find a pub. I remember walking through the doors and being so impressed with the friendliness of the staff and how inviting they were. Our plan was to have a few drinks before visiting the iconic Eiffel Tower.

Unfortunately, the plan was nullified once it was known that we had walked straight into a happy hour. To this day I am not convinced that it actually was happy hour, and still feel that the owner made a special exception for us. He probably knew what the exchange rate was at the time. We felt we were exactly where we needed to be as the owner continued to fill our cups with French delights. He switched on some lively music and kept asking us whether we would like to dance with some of the other guests at the pub. To be honest, my memory is vague on how those guests felt about the ordeal. I didn't hesitate and took advantage of the invitation. I loved it but the ladies didn't! The more the owner initiated the dancing, the more awkward the situation became for both parties. Eventually we all settled for staying hydrated, and I successfully avoided a charge of harassment. I recall someone explaining to me that this was not the Moulin Rouge.

After five happy hours at the pub, we only just made it back in time to join our tour group. We had completely missed the Eiffel Tower experience, but it was all worth it. Spending time with my friends, laughing and being silly was special. I realised how lucky I was to be able to spend time with these incredible people while also getting to meet new friends. It was simple, harmless fun, playing out in one of the most iconic cities in the world. The beauty is in the simplicity of it all. It was an ordinary day for most locals, while we were having a blast in an average pub with great people. It became a memory of great height and depth, that nurtured our longing for adventure. So simple and yet so significant.

***

It was 2015 and I was on honeymoon with my beautiful wife Danielle. We found ourselves in majestic Thailand, a country with spectacular natural wonders. Whilst staying in Karon, a small coastal town close to the hustle and bustle of Patong in Phuket, we decided to book a boat trip to some of the nearby islands. The trip was called the VIP Six Island Experience, and included the famous Maya Bay.

On this trip I met a scrawny young man with a bright smile that could light up a room. He was born and raised in Thailand and arrived at the scene of departure with an extraordinary amount of energy. He was authorised as the skipper of our boat and led the way to the abundantly beautiful islands while also doubling up as the tour guide. This man had so much spark that it was infectious. We all stood in awe as he moved around the boat effortlessly, doing everything in his power to make our trip as enjoyable and special as possible. He was easy to talk to and had great stories, even with his broken English, but I will remember him most for his cheerful spirit. There was always time for a laugh, often at the expense of the other crew members.

He was a simple fellow who didn't allow himself the time to stress too much about trivial things of little importance. He told us stories of sea gypsy ocean dwellers and how they lived off these islands. A standout tale was how they anticipated the infamous tsunami tragedy which hit the country a few years earlier. Apparently, because they lived in the oceanic wilderness, they were able to tell from the water levels that something was out of place. He told us how they tried to warn the government but were ignored as they were seen as the outcasts of society. We all know what happened next, and after the tsunami they were given reconciliation by being officially recognised as Thailand citizens. The story reminded me of God's miraculous ability to bring something good out of tragedies like the tsunami. I was so happy to hear how they were vindicated.

Our tour guide, who became my new hero, continued with enthusiasm as he turned up the throttle to reach the next island. At the next pit stop the man started shouting like a monkey, and I could relate for obvious reasons. Some people value degrees in literature, but this man had learned to comprehend the local monkey lingo. He kept screaming for the monkeys to come out and make a special appearance for us - and they did, emphatically. He told us that these were the only monkeys in the country that could swim, and he proved it by tossing food in the water. Relentlessly, they would swim to pick up the food and return to shore for a tropical feast.

Next on the agenda was snorkelling and we took a well-deserved and very refreshing splash in the natural aquarium created by these spectacular Phuket islands. The skipper jokingly mentioned that this stop was where Nemo from the Walt Disney movie hung out. He could probably smell my infatuation as we moved under water, where he quickly pointed me in Nemo's direction. It took about two minutes before we witnessed the famous fish swimming in the colourful coral. Nemo and all of his doppelgangers would hide in the ocean plantation, after which the skipper would go up and brush it, and all of them would emerge collectively. It was a simple stroke of local knowledge that would bring the utmost joy to any Travelling Monkey Lion visiting these beautiful waters.

It was time to make our way back to the mainland, and we all sat in silence as we attempted to take in the last few moments of the day. I grabbed Danielle's hand and smiled, simply content. The sun was setting and the cooler temperature was a relief to all of us. Needless to say, by the end of the trip, the tour guide and I were best friends. I decided to ask him a few questions about his life. Specifically, I wanted to know what an average day looked like for him, with my own preconceived answer in mind. I was enviously thinking that he was living the dream.

Here is his response. I'm going to paraphrase it. He said that in Thailand it is not easy to get a good job, so he moved to Phuket from his hometown as it was the only place with opportunities where he felt he could make a decent living. At least he could speak English, which made it a lot easier for him to find work. He started on this boat as a crew member and the skipper was kind enough to help him with his English. He spoke English to everyone and made a lot of friends from all over the world. Every morning he would wake up very early in order to get to the docks at 5:00 am. This happened even in poor weather, as people want to visit the islands every day. His day ended at 6:00 pm, only after cleaning the boat. He smiled and nodded, saying that he loved his job and enjoyed making friends. He went on, telling me about one event that illustrates his kindness and humility.

Once he made a friend from Russia who was on this very boat excursion. A few weeks later, the man came to him and asked for help. The Russian fellow had lost his passport and had no money to return home. The skipper took him into his home, shared his rice with him and taught him how to speak Thai. It was like having a baby who had to learn everything from birth, he said, laughing while he pulled up another one of the ropes hanging over the boat. He went on to say that the Russian worked with them until he had enough money to return back home. Not too long ago, the Russian came back and visited him and his family. He said they were all still great friends.

I was stunned. It was hardly what I had expected, and a very far reach from the dream-image I had painted of his life. I felt a bit ashamed, embarrassed, and even gutted. I often complain about trivial things. When I remind myself not to, it doesn't take long before the intense pace of everyday life pulls me back into that dangerously self-destructive mindset, a negative thought pattern. I was grateful for the truth which the Lord blessed me with that day. He definitely used this man's story to give me some divine perspective on the beauty of simplicity, and the power in living your best life for others. My Thai friend gave me more than just a boat trip, he gave me new-found truth. The beauty lies in living simply, enjoying what you have and what you do, and not focusing all your energy on what you want, but on what you have.

On all three of these trips, travelling certainly did raise a curtain in my mind's view, revealing valuable lessons that I will carry with me for the rest of my life. I consistently remind myself of these truths while living a busy life with high demands. Keep on discovering these truths when venturing into the unknown - the rewards cannot be measured. I had found the pure joy associated with simplicity. It was proven to me whilst on safari, on the stairs of a beautiful monument, and on the speedboats of Thailand.

CHAPTER 4

CROSS-DRESSING

The critical ability to have fun and not take ourselves too seriously can so easily be neglected. It is a key ingredient to travelling the world, as there will be many incidents where you will fall short or might have made a planning error. Not everything works out the way you planned, and you must be able to smile when life throws you a curveball or two.

Travelling can help with fostering the ability to not sweat the small things. It makes you realise how small you are and how insignificant our worries and anxieties can be. It all comes down to humility and letting go of our prideful nature. The Bible tells us that whatever is in our hearts will flow from our mouths. The Word also says that all earthly matters are vanity, a chase after wind, and should be seen for what they are - trivial.

It was 2006 and my friends and I were touring through Western Europe. We had arrived at our next destination, which was Austria. We were privileged to stop there for one day and night, which would include an exhilarating white river rafting adventure followed by a cross-dressing party later that evening. The irony was that the latter proved to be a much more intimidating prospect than the white-water rafting, leaving people scarred for life. I simply wasn't made to wear a skirt or a spaghetti tank top.

When we arrived at a pretty chilly white river rafting club in Tyrol, Austria, we all had to sit down for a brief on the rules of the river. We were surrounded by rolling hills which were mystically covered in crisp, white snow. The top white layer was like icing on a cake, a sweet topping with an aroma that made the adventure as surreal as the hot air leaving our mouths. The prospect of falling into the ice-cold waters of the nearby river became more evident as we endured the briefing. The tour guide gathered us together for the boat allocations and my heart started to pump vigorously in my chest. I'm not the adrenaline-rush type, and this was way out of my comfort zone. I got especially nervous when the guide referred to the water as "pretty cold", after which he gave us African boys a long and hard stare. The stare came with a sadistically sharp grin, and I knew then that we were in serious trouble.

It was a case of laughing or crying, and during this particular adventure we chose to laugh. It started long before the dodge boat expedition. I wasn't too body conscious at the time and was pretty adept at not taking anything too seriously. Getting into a wetsuit, though, brought about a bag full of problems. The guide firmly pointed out that a full wetsuit would be compulsory for all of us, in case we ended up in the icy waters during the trip. At this stage he was no longer grinning at all of us, but only at me. I knew I had no choice and pulled on the wetsuit with the same grit it takes a baby whale to leave the womb of its mother. Needless to say, there was a lot of laughter which literally broke the ice. No matter how hard I tried, the suit seemed to be too small. I eventually wobbled my way back to the group knowing that any chance I had of impressing the ladies was as unrealistic as using the toilet for the next few hours.

We managed to hit the water without too much of a splash. The drier the better, I thought as I nervously grabbed my rowing oar with pretentious vigour. I might even have grunted slightly as I pulled and bent for the first stroke. The small airtight boat started bouncing around slightly and we proceeded over the icy waters. There were probably around eight people per boat, which I thought was a bit of an ambitious fit - fit being the problem in every sense of the word.

The last dagger to my ego was when the guide mentioned that in the event of an emergency, we needed to brace ourselves between the seats of the boat. I asked my fellow crew members what to do in case we didn't fit, which led to a few more awkward laughs.

I ended up falling into the cold Austrian waters on more than one occasion, and the tour guide was right. It was freezing. Every time we hit a bump, I would fall off. Thank goodness for that wetsuit. On top of the obvious challenges of staying dry, there were a few occasions where the guide purposely caused some of us to fall overboard. I remember laughing so much I nearly drowned. I wasn't laughing at the fact that the water was cold or that he was throwing us overboard. I was laughing at myself. Once the ego subsided, it turned into an adventure I will never forget. Climbing back into the boat was a real challenge, and with a lack of upper body strength it could take several attempts. I wasn't impressing anyone, but it didn't matter as we were all having a great time.

As mentioned before, we had a cross-dress party planned for later that evening. The venue for this next adventure was in a blissful little backpacker's hostel situated in the middle of the impressive Austrian landscape. It was a calm atmosphere with a contradictory crazy theme planned for the evening's shenanigans. Fortunately, we'd all had so much fun during the day that we were in high spirits for the festivities. The first step in gaining access to the party involved each person finding someone from the opposite sex from whom they could borrow clothes. This was a very daunting task which should never be underestimated. Coming from a pretty stern South African background and being a long way from home, we found it hard to ask a lady if we could borrow her clothes. I kept thinking that if our dads could see us now, we would probably be on the first flight back to Johannesburg.

When we had accomplished that, and were all dressed up and ready to go, it would be fair to say that we all looked hideous. I'm so grateful that we didn't have Facebook or social media back then, as the photos weren't meant for the public eye. My friends and I made a deal that we'd keep this memory to ourselves. Yet here I am writing about it – sorry, guys. We had a blast that evening. I remember opening the dance floor with our female tour guide, who looked like a male bus driver.

The hostel's pub had a rule where you could receive an honorary certificate if you drank a certain number of their locally brewed shooters. Most of us had several of these by the end of the night but it had no effect. Honestly, the alcohol was so thinned out it was like drinking water. Nevertheless, I remember one of our fellow New Zealand travellers getting hammered on two litres of H2O. We laughed and had the best time during the party. We even played some tribal music CD we'd bought from a street vendor in London. Picture five men dancing like indigenous North American Indian women, all of them in skirts and tops while drinking water shots. Not taking life too seriously, not at all!

**

In January 2009, I found myself in one of the most iconic sports stadiums in the world. The Melbourne Cricket Ground (MCG) in Australia is a global cricketing fortress and a definite bucket list item for any sports fanatic. I was visiting a very good friend of mine and she managed to book us two tickets for a One Day International match between South Africa and Australia. The stadium has a capacity of 90,000 spectators, and if that doesn't create enough of an atmosphere, the rich history found in the iconic player statues of some of the greatest cricketers will leave you with a true sense of awe. The Australian heat in January is quite the opposite of the icy river rafting waters of Austria. Temperatures can reach over

40 degrees in summer. Perfect weather for a great game of cricket between two very proud nations.

When I initially arrived in Australia, I met a few South Africans and Zimbabweans who had emigrated there. They were lovely people and it was such a pleasure to meet and get to know them. I really enjoyed spending time with them as they made me feel extremely welcome and definitely added a lot of value to my trip. I shared my excitement about the cricket with them two weeks before and managed to convince them to join us. They all seemed pretty keen at the time but as you know, that does not always guarantee that people will actually show up.

One of the greatest privileges of this adventure was that I was able to stay with a great friend who was also a local. She introduced me to all of her friends and showed me spectacular parts of the country. When travelling, remember to try and connect with friends from previous adventures or make arrangements to go and visit them in their countries. Return the favour if at all possible. It really is the best way to see a country.

We arranged to meet up with all the immigrants at the stadium. I was so pleased to hear that they would be joining us. The moment I saw them, fully kitted in their South African colours, I smiled and laughed with so much excitement. It was such a special moment. It felt as if my Lion Heart was going to jump out of my chest. I took it upon myself to conduct the cheerleading squad and we started singing famous South African songs from back home. We sang songs from our school days which you would typically use during sporting events. It was real verbal diarrhoea to support our boys in the middle. Spirits were high. Laughter was abundant.

The expat choir led by yours truly made its way to our seats, which formed part of the top half of the stadium. The seats were perfect and gave us a bird's eye view of the proceedings below. The stadium screamed ecstasy, with its vast depth and potential spectator count. It was by no means a sell-out but you could feel the potential of a Boxing Day MCG cricket match at full capacity. The stadium is well looked after and in beautiful condition. It is easy to find your way around and it has a secure and family-like atmosphere, something which should be associated with going to these kinds of events.

The energy brought by the enthusiastic crowd was transcendent and accompanied by a tangible festive spirit. We took loads of silly pictures, joked around and had some excellent banter with our Australian counterparts. We were dancing in the stands and singing with everything we had, to keep our beloved players on the field motivated. Then came the moment which we would never forget. It was a tight game and one could sense the tension in the air. The winner would only be decided in the final stages of the match - it literally came down to the last ball. We were loving every moment and soaking up as much as possible. We stared and held our breath. South Africa needed three runs off one ball for the win. Johan Botha (former South African player) stepped up to face the final delivery and struck the ball with perfect timing and precision. The ball soared straight back over the bowler's head and went over the boundary rope for four runs.

South Africa won and we screamed, laughed, hugged and cheered like never before. You simply don't get any closer than that. I remember not knowing whether I should cry or laugh - I was absolutely ecstatic and so too were my fellow expat friends. Even our Australian counterparts were happy for us and took the defeat gracefully.

That month in Australia taught me many important life lessons. I must point out that Australians in general - at least, the ones that I met - know how to have fun. The entire group of people and their families always seemed able to not take life too seriously. This is a definite shortcoming in my own ancestry. I tend to take life too seriously. Perhaps you have the same problem. Australians are blessed with a sharp sense of humour. At the time it was clear they had a very different outlook on life compared to a lot of people back home. Travelling to Australia gave me the opportunity to conduct some introspection on my own areas for improvement. This was possible only because I was prepared to travel at the time, and made it a priority.

The endless opportunities to learn through travelling have shaped my life in a significant way. I believe it can do the same for you. We live in a time where perfectionism and comparison have become the norm. We tend to miss out on the fun stuff as we continue to stare down the barrel of distractions caused by social media and other similar platforms. We forget what it feels like to laugh at ourselves as our subconscious marvels at the endless facades posted by others. When we are constantly filtering our life through the perfect lens of online status updates and uploads, we forget to allow ourselves to be human. We forget to laugh. We forget to foster a positive spirit.

Life is increasingly adding to the pressures on us, and our only means of escape lies in the ability to live offline and have fun in the moment. Next time you travel, make it a point to have fun. I know it sounds weird, but it really can be a conscious decision. Leave the phone in the hotel room and venture into the streets of the unknown. Travelling has taught me that we have the most fun when we connect and engage face-to-face with other people. Especially at cross-dressing parties.

CHAPTER 5

MONKEY LION LOVEMAKING

Being abroad is a recipe for falling in love with new worlds, their people, culture and natural surroundings. When we experience such a sensation, we grow at an intense and almost exponential rate. The perception around love and what you need most or look for in a partner is hugely shaped by travelling. It makes a massive impact on your opinion of what is important whilst on the journey of finding a lifelong partner. This is a massively important reason to travel. In my own life, I didn't understand the full picture of what real love was, and I would never have been able to if it wasn't for my experiences while travelling.

Travelling the world created the platform from which my sense of love and its various forms and expressions were developed. One of the main lessons that revealed itself to me over time was the significant difference between love and lust.

Lust is an ever-lurking reality shaped by a modern culture. Many young people get caught up in damaging worldly standards and often suffer the consequences. Fortunately, whilst meeting so many people I was able to realise the true meaning of the words "love" and "lovemaking". It changed me for the better and I have travelling to thank for it. Perhaps this is the next thing that you need to figure out in your life and if so, I would highly recommend travelling to help guide your path. Learning what you want in love and life is key. The ability to differentiate between lust, true love, the love of a friend, and innocent love can literally change the course of your life.

It was 2006 and I was four months into my United Kingdom gap year. I was working at a London bar called Barracuda, a South African-themed pub. At the same time, I had a South African housing agency, friends and roommates. This all clearly illustrates the comforts towards which I gravitated during that first year abroad. As mentioned, my dream of staying with several female Brazilian flatmates had long disappeared, especially when I faced the harsh realities of the daunting concrete jungle. The familiarities associated with home instinctively became a lot more appealing without me making any conscious decisions.

This particular week entailed a staff party as a means to wish our boss farewell. I worked at the bar with a very good friend of mine whom I knew from back home. We eventually became roommates and had each other's backs that entire year. The night of the staff party arrived and we arranged for a trip to the local gentlemen's club close to where we worked. One of our fellow colleagues, who was much older than us, recommended the spot and planned to meet us there. He was an incredibly good person despite the introduction I just gave you. In my mind he was and still is one of the coolest people I have ever met. He was a strongly built Portuguese guy with a witty personality. He was a man of his word and looked out for us in his own unique way.

The entire experience of going to our first strip club was incredibly disappointing. It turned out to be the opposite of what the world promises it to be. What seemed like a good idea at the time turned out to be a lesson I'll never forget. The world will fill your head with lies; don't believe them. Everything perceived to be of value which falters from the path of righteousness will damage you and leave you feeling empty. That night I looked around and saw the unmasked face of lust. I glanced at the audience, or "gentlemen", and could not help but notice a very empty, sad and pale look in their eyes. I felt a sense of hopelessness, guilt and shame.

What made the night even worse was that they seemed to enjoy shouting banter to my young friend and me. They obviously noticed that we were young and out of place. The uncomfortable environment screamed desperate cries of broken people coming together to indulge each other in their pool of sadness. It broke my heart and tainted my spirit. Fortunately, we didn't stay long and I remember trying to convince myself that it wasn't that bad. Our Portuguese friend had noticed our apprehension and suggested that we head to the staff gathering. He defended us a few times while amongst the vultures and gently nudged us away from trouble. The poor guy probably had it much worse than us!

Lust is dangerous and I think it is something that creeps up on men. It can take you on a dangerous ride where you only later realise how damaging it was to your character, heart and spirit. Lust is very different from lovemaking.

***

Still in 2006, the next adventure took place in Amsterdam, a city infamous for its red-light district. This time I found myself in a place where the objects of the desires of the flesh are more easily accessible than they are in most places I have been. Amsterdam was the final stop on our Western European tour. We ended up in an area well known for prostitution as well as the legalisation of marijuana. Walking in those streets was unlike anything I had ever experienced. The streets were lined with huge windows facing the roads. Some windows had a red light positioned at the top, which meant that there was a lady available for prostitution. A light shining down on a person being sold as an item is the ultimate portrayal of a world obsessed with consumerism gone horribly wrong. Sadly, these ladies would cause a huge commotion while standing behind these windows, the idea being to get the attention of potential customers. As I naively walked with the scent of young vulnerability, it looked as if some of them were ready to break down their windows.

Today I still struggle to rationalise what our group experienced and the severity of that exploitation. I managed to avoid entering any houses with red windows. We also saw blue windows, which denoted male prostitutes posing as women. The blue alternative option made it much easier to stay as far away from these windows as possible.

Images and actions that provoke lust can be found in any city and at any time. These triggers are probably more accessible online than ever before while millions hide behind their supposedly invisible anonymous online profiles. The reality of Amsterdam will stay with me forever and has given me a different perspective around the reality of what sits behind lust and the dangers thereof. Lust and love turned out to be very different.

We will now focus on the beauty of love, the opposite element to lust, and the one that has an everlasting ring to it. Most travellers are romantics at heart and I bet you might be too. Dreamers enjoy the idea of soulmates, unconditional love, and believe that we are all capable of finding inner peace with someone who can join us on our life journey. Remember, God is love, and that is a good place to start.

**

It was 2009. I remember how excited Danielle and I were to finally cross international borders together. Our first travel experience was initiated after we planned a short trip to visit one of South Africa's neighbouring countries. The beautiful, lush valleys of Swaziland are about 350 kilometres from our home town, a short and scenic four-hour drive from Pretoria.

Prior to the trip, I had been mesmerising Danielle - or most likely boring her - with many of my travelling stories. This trip would finally make it possible for us to share one of our own, and after asking her parents for permission we were set and ready to go. The plan was to cross the border in my Mazda 323, an old blue beauty that ran like the wind. My first car was experienced and perhaps even a little worn, but still capable, and willing to explore new terrains like nothing else on four wheels.

We were both hungry for an adventure and did our homework before the trip. We found suitable accommodation at a local backpackers' lodge in the Ezulwini Valley, called Lidwala Lodge. It was the first time ever that Danielle had been to one of these fine establishments, and she loved it. Backpackers' lodges tend to have the potential to be these magical hubs of diversity characterised by people with a common interest. We all love travelling. People from all over the world gather to debrief on their travel adventures, the core focus being all about meeting new people and exploring new places.

Unfortunately, some backpackers' lodges can be a little shady even when considering the purpose they serve - affordable travelling. I have been to one or two where we had to turn around before checking in. You might know exactly what I'm talking about... Luckily, this Swaziland treasure turned out to be one of the best backpackers' lodges I've ever stayed at. We were checked into a huge tented room which was engulfed by the distinct aroma of the African bush. It had that familiar canvas smell that only comes with camping. The tented room had a wooden balcony that extended our bushveld villa into an outside deck under the magnificent trees of the bush. We also had a stunning backdrop of high valleys situated behind the lodge.

All of this formed the perfect setting for our first co-travel experience. I was sure that we would someday drink cheers to this while sipping on our tea at our old-age home. It was beautiful, and I was so grateful that I got the opportunity to embark on something special like this with Danielle. It planted a seed for many more adventures, although ironically, we had no idea at the time what a significant step this was to be for our love journey.

Our first day in Swaziland naturally progressed to the number one tourist attraction in the area. The day trip that we booked included an excursion to a local village where we were transported back in time. The village life confronted us with a pleasant reminder of the simplicities associated with living with the absolute basics. The native Swazi people stayed in small tribal huts, dome constructions made of grass on frames of saplings. The village had no medical facilities but these where fortunately (or unfortunately) covered by the local *sangoma* (traditional medicine practitioner). I suppose it depends on how you look at it.

In the centre of the village, they had a basic fire pit which served as the communal kitchen. We learned that many of them still stayed in the village while others only wore their attire for the tourist show. Once the show was done, they would change back into their Nike and Adidas wear before heading back home. We didn't care too much as it seemed authentic enough, and we both felt it was an honest and pure way to earn a living.

The outing also included some traditional dancing and other festivities associated with ancient rituals. It was a wonderful display of fitness, charisma, flexibility and rhythm. It felt as if I was going to pull a hamstring simply by looking at what they were able to do with their bodies. They were giving high-flying kicks like Bruce Lee and screaming and shouting like Freddy Mercury, all combined into a flawless 30-minute performance. Their joy in performing was evident. They all synched perfectly, with excellent chorography which included movements from all body shapes and sizes, age groups and genders. I was relieved to see that they had their Nike and Adidas shorts on under the African skirts, otherwise the show would have been more like the one in London.

The members of the group were clearly very proud of their heritage, and their love for tradition was admirable. The love they had for their history and their people was pure and true. True love is more than just the love for your spouse, children and family. It is also about love for your heritage and culture. So often we are told that our traditions, heritage, and most importantly our faith, should be considered outdated. Swaziland proved this theory wrong. Travelling often reveals the lies told by the social circles around your comfort zone. You should always be proud of your heritage and prioritise your faith above everything else. It is the foundation of your existence and ultimately forms your core perception of true love. This precious love leads to purpose and inner peace.

True love comes in many forms and we need to be attentive to this when travelling, and reminisce around the source. Discovering things which we could not see or did not realise was the most precious part of that trip. We got to know each other on a totally different level and in a neutral setting.

Remember that God is the source of true and unconditional love. He is abounding in love and slow to anger, and nothing you can do will change His love for you. His love is all we need and the joy displayed by the villagers of Swaziland turned out to be a valuable reminder of this truth. True love is from and through God, and only once discovered can it be conveyed to others. My true love was right there, both in my heart, and with Danielle standing next to me. As we witnessed the dancers doing backflips, I did not think that she would again stand next to me six years later on our wedding day. The signs of true love were written in the Ezulwini Valley without us even realising it.

***

In 2006, I was having my farewell party after spending a year in London at a well-known southern hemisphere-themed pub called Walkabout. Unfortunately, my precious gap year had come to an end. It had probably been the best year of my life up to that point. Prior to the farewell extravaganza, I was responsible enough to transfer most of my savings back to South Africa and kept my last few pounds for the final couple of days before my return flight to the mothership.

On the evening of the farewell, as my friends started to arrive I was thinking how amazing it was to have so many new friends from different parts of the world. However, it was my new-found South African friends that had become more like family during the course of the year. When people travel together, it creates a unique bond that has the ability to bring you very close to each other in a short space of time.

There is a different love here, and it became evident as it resurfaced and confirmed some truths. The love of friendship is a key ingredient of happiness. It is only in community that we are able to live out the purpose of glorifying God through serving and fellowship with others.

There was a girl at the pub whom I really liked and my heart skipped a beat whenever I saw her. We use to hang out all the time. Low on confidence, I never had the guts to tell her how I felt, but I thought that a farewell might be an ideal platform. I decided that I had absolutely nothing to lose and that the worst (and most likely) case scenario would be that she might disappear and go into hiding until I left the country. Logically, and as many of us tended to do at the time, I attempted to draw courage from the bar. I was working my way through the last few pounds at an alarming rate. My friends were looking on with concern.

The night came to an end (thankfully) and I remember seeing her on the dance floor sharing a kiss with another guy. I should have known. She was way out of my league anyway, so naturally, as all mature men would do, I drank so much that I eventually got sick. I drowned in self-pity, but two friends stayed behind despite the horror show. They saw what had happened and knew that I would be crushed. I vaguely remember lying flat on my face at one of the tables at the pub. My concerned friend sat next to me and calmly suggested that it was time to catch a night bus home. It sounded like the best idea of the evening and we made our way to the bus station.

As I was walking back with the imprint of the table on my forehead, I realised that I had spent all my money. I had nothing left - not even a cent - and I still had two days to go before my flight. The spending money which I had convinced myself would be impossible to spend in one night went down the throats of the peers I was hoping to impress. This left me with a shortage of cash for food and transport. I complained to my friend about my heartbreak in a justifiable manner and then about the shortage of cash dilemma. He looked at me and generously gave me £30, which would be more than enough to cover my expenses. It even paid for my Pakistani haircut, which is worth a chapter on its own. I said "trim" not "short" and certainly not "round". Goodbye afro.

Not only did my friend sit with me until the end, but he also helped me over the final hurdle of this unequivocal adventure which was to shape my life in more ways than I could ever imagine. This is the lesson of love found in friendship. It can be very selfless and precious, and is key to travelling fearlessly. I respect solo travelling and envy those who have done so, but for me, sharing these experiences with friends is a priceless endeavour. It carries power and love that nourish and connect the soul. My friend showed me a different side to love that evening, and the farewell turned into a lesson in humility. There is simply nothing like the love of a friend.

***

We keep going in 2006. Love once again came to the fore, in a different form. We have covered lust, true love, the love of a friend, and in Italy I was about to discover the magic of innocent love. I found myself in the fairy-tale city of Florence after visiting iconic cities like Rome and Venice. The story forms part of the European adventure which I have spoken about previously. I was still dressed in male clothing, but nevertheless en route to the Austrian cross-dress party which I did not yet know was to take place a few days later.

A group from our tour party was about to embark on a pub crawl evening arranged by our operator. The lights of Florence were captivating; the city landscapes are like a picture-perfect painting, sculpted for the indulgence of the eye. The ancient buildings are those you remember seeing on television as a child. It is a truly magical city filled with rich history and a sense of mystery. The Arno River is at the centre of it all, flowing quietly while adding the final piece of majesty. There are cathedrals everywhere, and building structures so amazing that you feel privileged to lay hands on them. The streets were filled with washing lines on balconies, while you could hear the acoustic sounds of the musicians busking next to restaurants. All of this while smelling the aroma of authentic Italian cuisine.

My friend had apparently developed some really deep feelings for one of the ladies who went out with us that evening. I'm still not sure if it is possible to develop deep feelings for someone in just two weeks, but that was what he said. I recall seeing how good they were together. The two of them had a unique bond, and like the city it was pretty special. It was as if they just got each other. I remember them laughing at jokes which none of us understood. They basically had a tour on their own – not telling anyone about the mischief, the practical jokes, and their obvious but innocently hidden agenda. The truly unique part was the platonic love between them.

We had a fantastic evening and ended up at several different venues as per the schedule. We finally finished our itinerary at a club with a smoking section the size of a shoe box. We eventually huffed and puffed our way out of there and decided to call it a night. I noticed that on the way back to camp these two were holding hands for the very first time. It was Monkey Lion lovemaking at its best. Due to unforeseen circumstances, they had to share a tent that night. I can confirm that this was not due to their own doing, but rather because the lust aspect got the better of their roommates. We all knew the circumstances and had a burning desire to find out what would transpire.

The next morning, my friend told me that they went to bed that night and lay next each other in separate sleeping bags, filling the space between them by simply holding hands; and that is exactly how they fell asleep. Love in its purest and most innocent form can be a powerful thing. Whilst travelling in Florence, I saw a beautiful city but an even more beautiful display of innocent love.

The various shapes and forms of love are ready for you to discover. Find your own truth. It cannot be taught, but only learned through experience. Whether it is uncovering the lies of lust or finding the truth of true love, it is there for you to find. What does Monkey Lion lovemaking mean to you?

CHAPTER 6

YOU SHOULD HAVE
BEEN BLACK

One of the things that I enjoy most about travelling is the fact that you get to discover new things about yourself. Not only that, you also get to make peace with the things you're not, and solidify things you might already know about yourself. The discovery of self is key. There is something about being abroad that opens your heart to discovering these new things, making you more aware of the characteristics that make you who you are.

It was 2010 and we were at the final stop on our southern African adventure. We had reached the beautiful country of Mozambique, a tropical paradise situated on the East Coast of southern Africa. It is one of those places enriched with palm trees and long stretches of beach, a location typically associated with travel agency brochures advertising honeymoons or cocktails in the sun.

Upon arrival, we were engulfed by a festive island vibe accompanied by the smell of ocean breeze and freshly baked bread. It was an invigorating and intriguing morning as we started to explore the surroundings. The country is a former Portuguese settlement and this shows in the spicy chicken dishes advertised in most restaurants and cafés along the streets. It is amazing how entrenched the European influences are in various African countries. The influences from the past are still very evident in their architecture, food, language and culture.

We stayed in Inhassoro, a fishing port in the Inhambane Province. We were camping in one of the local spots and found ourselves less than 200 metres away from the bar as well as the beach. This turned out to be an unprecedented combination, as we indulged in the infamous Mozambique delicacy, a rum and raspberry drink. It tasted so good that it made my friend swim naked in the ocean in the middle of the night. After losing a simple bet with one of the female tourists, he was forced to venture into the ocean without any clothes or inhibitions. We all stood in disbelief as Mozambique was exposed to something no country should ever see. I recall making a few rugby-like tackles on some of our new friends, and to this day I'm not sure why. I can only attribute this behaviour to the friendly barman who kept our glasses full as well as the intricacies found in the stunning environment.

The evening didn't stop there, as we moved to one of the local taverns for the after party. By this stage, sanity had prevailed and we opted for local beer rather than the infamous rum and raspberry drink. Talk about grace. This brought some stability to proceedings. However, we still had enough liquid courage to try our chances at a self-arranged dance-off competition with the locals. African people in general are gifted dancers with great rhythm. All the local taverns have huge speakers from which they belt out their music all night long. I remember standing next to one of them and actually feeling the vibrations in my chest. I love a good dance-off competition and pride myself on my moves, or the lack thereof. I told the locals that my hips had a mind of their own. This was only to save me from the inevitable embarrassment to follow. I'm pleased to report that I got a much-appreciated vote of confidence following the dance-off. All the tavern locals unanimously agreed that I should have been black. What an amazing compliment! It took my dance-off confidence to new heights.

Mozambique reminded me how much I love people. I can honestly say that the trip instilled a new longing in me to never stop meeting new people. I learned that it fuels me and gives me confidence, to mingle with different people from different backgrounds. Whilst at school we moved around a lot and I remember begging my parents to keep me in the same school regardless. I was scared to leave my friends behind and felt nervous when walking into a room where I didn't know anybody. You might be able to relate. Travelling has helped me to get over the fear of meeting new people and being vulnerable in environments where I didn't know anyone. I rediscovered my love for people while travelling, and now have no issue with walking into a room where I am the new guy or a stranger. In fact, I honestly enjoy it and sometimes crave it. That is the power of discovering new things about myself when travelling - while also realising that I should have been black.

**

In 2006 I found myself on a bus to Dublin, Ireland. I was accompanied by two of my best friends, the twins, whom I met in London that same year. One thing you can be sure of is that when you travel with these boys, you're in for a good time. This was a particularly special occasion as we were on our way to watch our beloved Springboks (the South African national rugby team) take on the Irish in their back-yard. When I was growing up, I was always fascinated with sport, and to me this seemed like a dream come true. Even though the bus left from London, it was packed with only South African expats and travellers. The excitement was electrifying and I remember the tangible atmosphere in the bus. There was pure elation and nervous excitement, which is often produced when on adventures you could only have imagined. If you enjoy sport, I would highly recommend that you plan your next trip around a sporting event that you would love to watch. Similarly, you can look at options for concerts or music festivals if that is your thing.

Given the excitement, the last thing I wanted to think about was a mild flu lurking in the background. I could feel that my throat was scratchy and my nose was getting stuffy - pretty much the opposite feeling of elation. A real mood killer. I kept telling myself that I'd be fine and decided to try and focus on the trip.

As we approached our accommodation, the tour guide asked who opted for which hostel. To put it simply - there were two options - a cheap one and a more expensive one. He started with the more affordable package, the twins and I looked at each other and slowly raised our hands. Initially we felt a bit embarrassed, but fortunately the shame was quickly overpowered by a huge cheer from the back of the bus. It was a group of fanatic Springbok supporters who also opted for the "good value for money" option.

Following the loud cheer, we were invited to the back of the bus. This had happened to me before, and it wasn't good. I nervously made my way to the cool kids. All three of us had to kneel down and take a squirt of their self-made sherry gun. The armed occupant had a bag strapped around his shoulders with two thin pipes connecting to twin squirt guns. Another set of twins? Can you believe the irony? No doubt these guys came prepared for whatever the Irish were going to throw at us that weekend. It was a masterfully crafted weapon specifically made to combat the cold and wet weather conditions, or any other discomfort for that matter.

That evening, we checked in briefly and made our way to a street lined with some of the most vibrant pubs in Dublin. Everyone seemed in good spirits as we made our way to The Temple Bar. This is a very well-known pub and somewhat of an oasis for foreign Springbok supporters. Here the twins and I got the surprise of a lifetime, as all the Springbok rugby players who were not involved in the match the next day arrived at the venue.

The myths and legends around The Temple Bar turned out to be true. It really was a local hang-out place for any South African travelling in Ireland. This was an incredible opportunity as we had a chance to spend time with some of our heroes. My personal favourite was Butch James and although he was a relatively new member of the side, he later became one of the Springbok players who would win the World Cup in France the following year.

Despite all the action that was going on, I was constantly aware of those flu-like symptoms that became apparent when we left London. The wet and cold weather wasn't helping and I woke up the next morning with my voice still being held captive at The Temple Bar. I could hardly get a word out. The first stop we made was at the pharmacy, before we eventually left for the famous Lansdowne Road rugby stadium.

This was one of the most iconic rugby stadiums in the world at the time. As you approach the stadium you immediately notice the old gates and signs. It was all purposefully left in its original state to create that unique historical atmosphere that the stadium is known for. In the corner of the stadium there sits an old pub that has probably been around for decades. I could just imagine how the fans of old would go there for a drink in their coats and hats before their beloved Irish team made their way onto the field. The stadium is small and intimate, which made the atmosphere around the park denser than the fog surrounding our bodies on that cold autumn evening.

Two sore-throat tablets later, and the twins and I were having a beer in the old corner bar. We were not dressed in suits or hats, but neon orange underground construction pants and all the Springbok attire we owned. We looked awesome! The match also celebrated the Springbok team's fiftieth year of existence. The players were dressed in the same kit design the Springboks wore in their first international match fifty years earlier. It included black shorts with green jerseys and a white collar - distinctly different to the usual green and gold. I remember watching these matches on television as a young boy, and listening to the national anthems of Ireland, Scotland and Wales before the game started. It got me every time. Hence it was an emphatic moment when I stood there in the flesh, able to witness a full stadium singing the Irish national anthem. As their voices roared above the iconic stadium, I was nostalgically longing for mine, which was still missing in action.

The match kicked off and I was really feeling sick by this stage. I started to realise that I wasn't going to be able to push on for much longer. I needed to rest. I tried my very best not to let it get to me, but I was inevitably feeling tired. Honestly, I just wanted some dry clothes and a warm bed. The worst part was that the Springboks were losing the contest, and as the Irish ticked over the scoreboard I was also losing my match against this bug.

Travelling is definitely not all sunshine and roses. We often go through difficulties while seeking adventure. Most travellers will know exactly what I'm referring to and we each have our own unique stories relating to challenging situations whilst abroad. It forces us to learn new things about ourselves. We tend to think that we are indestructible and that we are capable of pushing through anything. Some of us are just too afraid to admit our vulnerability. I was one of those people in 2006. Not anymore.

Later that evening we went for a walk through the vibrant street again, to mourn the loss we had suffered at the hands of the Irish. I managed one Guinness before requesting an escort to our cheap hostel, and when I say escort, I mean one of the twins. He walked with me all the way to the hostel before going back to join his brother - a true friend. That night was long and hard. I must have consumed about half of Dublin's flu tablet supplies without managing to break the fever. After a year of living like there was no tomorrow, the reality kicked in hard that I was only human. It was a hard lesson that travelling taught me, and unlike in the experience in Mozambique, there was no dancing. I had to face the harsh realities of an unhealthy lifestyle that was damaging my body. The flu was a result of months and months of negligence.

God gives us guidelines through His scriptures on how to live a life of freedom and prosperity, and mine was simply not aligning. I learned that I was not indestructible. It is a lesson that no one can teach you. You wouldn't listen to that nonsense. It is something you need to experience for yourself. Even if I was a black Mozambican dancing in the streets of Dublin, there was no escaping the jaws of self-destruction that evening.

***

It was 2006 and I was slowly making my way to the top of the Alps in Switzerland. I found myself on a cable car carrying us to the top of this spectacular mountain. We'd had our first party on the European tour the night before, and I had decided to show off my unofficial so-called black rhythmic heritage. The splendour of the environment was nothing less than breathtakingly beautiful with tall mountains proudly surrounding us. It was as if they were dipped in a bowl of snow. As you glanced over the mountains you could see a white blanket stretching over the enormous landscape. I had never seen snow before, and being able to experience that moment is a privilege I will hold dear forever.

The town which we stayed in was called Lauterbrunnen, and it had everything you would associate with a story from a children's book about magic, kingdoms, princesses and waterfalls. The area is lush green with natural water features falling down from all corners of the Alps. The streets are characterised by wooden taverns and smoky chimneys. It felt surreal, and almost too much to comprehend and truly appreciate.

My friends were especially excited because they were about to ski and snowboard, a highlight on our itinerary which they were looking forward to. I knew that I had the balance capabilities of a hippo-ballerina and that snowboarding and skiing would make me the villain of this children's book. I opted to stay indoors, and explore the ice castle on the way to the top.

The day doubled up as an opportunity to make amends for the disgrace of the night before. I had embarrassed myself in the worst possible way. I'd felt I had a good opportunity to sneak a kiss from a fellow traveller at the wooden cabin party the previous night. We ended up walking all the way to one of Lauterbrunnen's waterfalls. To this day I still claim that it is one of the most romantic spots in the world, and that I had no choice but to try and sneak a pash. These are the party stories no one ever tends to tell - the stories of embarrassment and misery that so often result from overindulgence. It is a hard and sometimes costly lesson.

The build-up was the least brutal part, and the trek to glory was everything you would expect before a romantic gesture. Our feet were breaking through long tall grass as we impulsively decided to change our course to a self-found nonconventional shortcut. You could hear the water tumbling down in the far-off distance as we continued to approach the waterfall. The moment for the perfect kiss was agonisingly close. Even the stars played their part in the clear sky above us. I could feel it. I dragged my feet the last few hundred metres, waiting for the crowd to move along as I took my chance while catching my breath.

But she politely declined and mumbled something along the lines of "we won't be kissing this trip". And so the most embarrassing moment of rejection the world has ever seen was born. My ego fell further and harder that any breathtakingly beautiful waterfall in the world. I walked away in shame on what had to be the longest trek of my life. I had no one to blame but myself, and in hindsight it set me up for another valuable lesson about myself.

I have the unique ability to take any bad situation and turn it into something good. I naturally broke the awkwardness and carried on as if nothing had happened for the remainder of the trip, humour being incredibly important to my attempt at salvation. This is actually really hard to master. Ironically, I became really good friends with that same lady, and it made for a good story.

Travelling gives you confidence. It helps you to believe in yourself and teaches you not to worry too much about the small things. Once you are confronted with how big the world really is, it immediately makes the big things in your life look really small. Had this happened to me in high school, I probably would have never spoken to this girl again. Fleeing would have been the preference instead of facing the situation.

Travelling taught me about rejection, and that I was strong enough to handle it. There are lessons you need to learn about yourself. It is part of the personal growth journey which is key for you to live your best life. Whether it is the fact that you thrive when meeting new people, or that you have your limitations, or that you are stronger than the disappointments that life throws at you, it needs to be learned. It can only be done while God accompanies you into ventures that break your routine and destroy the limited outlook fostered by your repetitive surroundings.

Who knows? Perhaps you also need a dance-off to discover that you too should have been black. You might have experienced a trip where you bravely stared death in the face. Or perhaps a few rejections were needed to make you realise that you can make the best out of any situation. I hope you like cheese, because I'm going to say this: travel far enough and you might find yourself.

CHAPTER 7

RISKY BUSINESS

This chapter is all about taking faith-fuelled risks and making sure that you don't miss a moment to learn, explore and grow. If it was easy, everyone would do it. You simply need to be prepared to take calculated and worthwhile risks once in a while. This is particularly important when travelling, as most people prefer to stay away from the path of exploration. Society will push for materialism or consumerism, but travelling Monkey Lion investments run on a different ideal. Difficult to pinpoint and not necessarily tangible, the return on investment relies solely on life experience. Personal growth and life-changing encounters with people from different backgrounds and cultures is the ultimate reward. No one will be able to take that away from you. It is a sound investment that becomes a handy tool for the future.

Faith is based on the principle of believing in something we cannot see. This principle forms the foundation from which the risk can be embarked on. My faith in God has equipped me to take calculated risks in pursuit of the eternal treasures found in travelling and adventure. I believe that God is ultimately in control of our life, purpose and destiny. The Lord has been my foundation for as long as I can remember, and as I get older, I realise more and more how dependent I am on His love and grace. Looking back at some of the decisions I have made on my journey, I do sometimes feel a bit embarrassed. However, due to His unconditional love things have always worked out for the better, making every risky business venture well worth the investment.

It was 2008 and I found myself in my second year at the University of Pretoria. My love for travel had only grown since my gap year in London, and I had many dreams and ambitions to continue travelling the world. The problem with being a student, though, was that you had all the time in the world for travelling but very limited resources for doing so. However, I was determined and knew that I wanted to continue travelling as much as possible. I even knew where I wanted to go, and was specific when setting my next goal. The destination in mind was Australia. I had some really wonderful Australian friends whom I had met in London and they had offered me a place to stay when visiting!

All I needed was to get the funds for a plane ticket and a little bit of budget for spending. The plan seemed flawless and simple, but to be honest it was a lot more complicated. But I wasn't going to allow any obstacle to withhold me from the next continent I had set my heart on, and was committed to finding a way to make things happen. The clear and obvious obstacle was my lack of finances. I'm sure many readers can relate, but please know that this is something you can definitely overcome if you set your mind to it. There are plenty of online resources for available options around travelling on a budget. I encourage you to explore these when you get a chance.

The trip to Australia was to be my first travel experience since my gap year. At the time my options were very limited and my only chance to venture across the Atlantic Ocean would depend on the money I had received from my student loan. I was going to take a substantial amount of study fees and use that to visit my friends in Australia. This would go against all reason and rational thinking and there was no doubt that it would be a leap of faith. Risky business. At the time I knew that I was taking a risk which would significantly impact the next year. However, at the same time I felt that everything would work out as I had faith and a plan.

The idea was to work while studying the following year, which would make up for using the money to travel. It was hard but it worked like a charm. I think we are allowed to be bold, especially when we are young with less responsibility. I also feel that we should try and hold on to this sense of freedom for as long as possible, if not forever. I don't think that taking risks should ever become redundant. If anything, it should simply be more calculated. Timing is important; and my responsibilities were minimal, which gave me the leverage I needed. It was risky but worth it.

I learned more about myself in that one month in Australia than I did during my three years on campus. I saw so many beautiful landscapes and landmarks, including Apollo Bay, The Melbourne Cricket Ground, the Twelve Apostles and the St Kilda beach fronts in Victoria. I saw the impressive Blue Mountains, Sydney Harbour Bridge and the Sydney Opera House, and played "Hey Cow!" on the ultimate road trip from Melbourne to Sydney. I also met wonderful people who have had a significant impact on my life. One friend in particular went out of her way to make it a once-in-a-lifetime experience. She looked after me and spoiled me in a massive way, and I will forever be grateful to her.

Everything worked out more than fine. I got back from the trip, got a job as an au pair, and managed to pass and pay for my third year studies. The leap of faith paid off and the risky investment exceeded all my expectations. Not everyone gets the opportunity to travel, and those who do usually take a few risks along the way. Always have a sound plan but be willing to swim upstream from time to time - it is not called risky business for nothing.

***

In 2006, around mid-May, I was tired of feeling stuck in a classic situation of being overworked and underpaid. I'm sure you know exactly what I'm talking about - we've all been there. I'd been working as a waiter and bartender in London for the past three months. It was not the easiest of jobs, with the difficult hours that are a trademark of an ungrateful industry.

The pub culture in England is a huge deal and regular late-night outings are a massive part of everyday life. There is nothing like a fully packed London pub watching a live football match, whether it is during the week or on weekends.

On the bright side, this pub-life chapter of my gap year was great for a period of time and allowed me to meet loads of wonderful people. I'd been working with a bunch of Polish beauties and some days it felt like we were on the set of a modelling shoot. The unfortunate and distinct communication barrier was partly because I was in awe but also because of their limited use of the English language.

I remember writing cheesy love poems and sticking them up on the pub wall, having cheap lunches with the Brazilian kitchen staff, joking around with intoxicated guests and carrying kegs of beer until my lower back went into a frenzy. We had built good friendships with a few local customers and they would often stop by for a cold pint after work. It was a coming-of-age time for me and I was intrigued with the exciting English pub culture associated with the bustling city.

The biggest obstacle of my occupation, however, was that I was simply not making enough money to travel and see more countries. The pay was based on the standard minimum wage and depended solely on the number of hours you were given to work in a particular week. I had dreams and aspirations to visit the rest of Europe and discover iconic places like Paris, Amsterdam, Rome, etc. The reality was that we could hardly afford rent, and I knew that it was time for a leap of faith which would involve some risky business.

My options for job opportunities were very limited and I couldn't really do much given my novice background. But despite the odds against me, I remained determined and kept my ears open for possible vacancies. There was also a sense of faith and I was positive that God would provide the appropriate opportunity at the right time. My faith in the Lord was justified in June when one of my South African friends mentioned that he would be able to get us work at a security company called Pegasus. However, there was a caveat which forced me to take a leap of faith. It became apparent that in order to move forward, I had to quit my bartender job so I could attend the security training program.

The training meant that I would need to attend a two-week course. This made it impossible to stay at the pub and I had no choice but to put in my first resignation. It was disappointing to witness the cold goodbye from management, but I suppose this was the first step in preparing me for the sting of the corporate world. It was disappointing that my praises were sung whilst I was a resource, yet I became a complete nuisance once I mentioned that it was time to move on. The harsh reality sank in that in this world everyone is replaceable, so much so that someone else could easily fill the shoes of an overweight poetic bartender. Who would have thought?

I consider myself a loyal person and despite the hostile farewell, it still felt like a tough goodbye. It wasn't easy and it was risky, but I knew that the new job would give me the opportunity to make enough money to travel. I was making a decision which would be in my best interest and I simply had to disregard the disappointment it would bring to others, people who valued my input, attitude and services. Perhaps you needed to hear that today. I want to encourage you to take the calculated risk and accept that your employer will get over you leaving. More quickly than you would like to admit. If leaving opens up new opportunities to travel, then go for it, especially if the calculation makes sense.

What followed was two weeks of mellow training which wasn't too intense, to say the least. I can't image the Special Forces being similar in anyway. The most hectic thing we had to do was a role play scenario where someone was entering the building without permission. I was the trespasser and had to shout at my fellow future colleague, who "refused to let me in". My instructor was very impressed with my performance, which would be more suited for a drama rehearsal than a security training course. Nevertheless, we got through it all and completed the course after writing a final exam at the end of the two weeks, in which the trainer whispered the answers to us in a very non-discreet way.

This resulted in the ultimate waiting game, as we would be called in and placed at a site when one became available. In retrospect, this was the most appropriate preparation for my new career in security - mastering the art of watching the clock. It was several weeks before I heard anything from them about where I would be deployed, and what clock I was watching! The wait was a lot longer than anticipated and the funds in my bank account were slowly decreasing as the temperatures increased that summer. It is safe to say I was hot under the collar, with anxiety levels rising exponentially.

I was running out of savings at a rapid rate, and it eventually took me to a point where I wasn't able to pay rent for a couple of weeks. I was in a desperate situation and the housing agency eventually demanded my passport as a means to ensure that I would pay what I needed to and not just leave. Things got really scary fairly quickly. I was a young man in a foreign country without a job, passport, Polish girlfriend or money. All I had was an afro, love handles and a few good friends. This was no drama rehearsal and I was in the midst of some real risky business.

Just before resorting to the dreaded call back home with instructions to rob a bank and send some money, the good news came through. God provided once again. I got a phone call from the security company, who wanted to know when I would be able to start and whether I would be keen to work at a site in central London. Without hesitation I responded that I could start that same day - which was exactly what they wanted to hear. The risky business based on the faith of a naive young man paid off and everything worked out perfectly.

I started working at the site in June and booked the European tour a few months later. The tour included an itinerary which catered for stops at all the well-known magical cities I longed to experience, the ones I so desperately wanted to visit. It was on that same tour that I met lifelong friends whom I visited in Australia a few years later. The tour also unexpectedly doubled up as the starting point for another risky business story, as featured in this chapter. The investment paid off in abundance.

Faith coincides with the characteristic of patience. Having faith is all about truly trusting God, with a complete sense of letting go. The notion is easier said than done but can be cultivated when we're forced into situations where we have no other choice. These situations are often encountered when travelling. Are you banging against doors that are locked? Are you anxious and fearful when losing the feeling of being in control? If so, then I can relate. I'm sure you will agree that it is not a sustainable, healthy way to progress through life. We need a solution.

Faith can be described as believing in the things we cannot see. It is interesting that when we encounter daily incidents of highly favoured yet unlikely events, we often automatically choose to see them as coincidence rather than divine intervention. Faith is all about believing that God has your back and the story of your life is in His capable hands. One of the most beautiful things about travelling is that you will need to make hard choices in certain situations. All decisions can be calculated but there are no guarantees for success. Faith is key, and accepting that it is risky is part of the process. Taking risks increases self-esteem and makes you aware of how courageous you truly are when faced with adversity. Make those decisions with a bold faith and pray for God's hand to be over your decisions. Travelling accelerates personal growth through various means and taking risks in unknown environments is certainly one of them.

One practical and easy decision you can make today is to start planning your next adventure. It might cost more than most would deem acceptable, but if you work out the pros and cons and believe that this is what you need in order to grow and discover yourself, then why not take the risk?

CHAPTER 8

LEARN WHAT YOU DON'T WANT

As you might have already gathered, it is evident that travelling forms a crucial part of your self-discovery process, allowing you to learn more about life, people and the world in general. It provides immeasurable clarity about yourself by giving you new perspective when experiencing different things. You will be confronted with unique situations tailored to provide you with golden opportunities to learn more about who you are. The natural push towards the unknown crosses the boundaries of our comfort zones and automatically creates an opportunity for emotional and spiritual growth. Through these life-giving experiences I have noted the importance of being exposed to situations where I realised what I didn't want.

There are many messages that invade our privacy in the phenomena of digital and social media platforms. Finding silence and solitude by drowning out the noise is a constant battle, and it makes it extremely difficult to determine what you don't want in your life. You will find that travelling inevitably provides you with many scenarios from which you can observe your surroundings objectively, taking you out of your situation to allow you to actually see it for what it is. This is often simply because you're a visitor and there are no preconceived notions or bias connotations. People will be your clearest indicator and guide whilst speeding up the process of determining what you don't want in life. And there are many things you shouldn't want, and should therefore avoid and disregard.

It is 2006 and I'm taking you back to the frisky town of London, the city that never sleeps. I found myself at the Lord's cricket ground, which is known as the home of cricket. This weekend I would be living out an itinerary that any sport fanatic would find magical.

When I arrived at the historical ground, there were numerous familiar scenes from my days of watching cricket on television. The tradition and the atmosphere offered an alluring effect that is hard to comprehend. The people were well-mannered and seemed fairly diplomatic as the teams engaged in a county match between two well-known cricket clubs.

I took some time to have a look around the facilities, and found myself in the cricket warehouse situated on the ground. I spent hours taking in the smell of authentic English willow; hundreds of cricket bats were waiting to be bought, oiled and knocked-in before falling into the hands of a batsman.

My roommate and I took our seats and I remember watching former Pakistan leg-spinner Mustaq Ahmed make his way to the bowling crease. I was there to witness the legend himself, bowling at Lord's, in a county match on a Sunday afternoon.

The day before, I was treated to the contrasting atmosphere of wild men chanting at the famous Stafford Bridge, home of the popular English football club Chelsea. Unlike the short queues at the food stalls of Lord's, there I saw long beer queues of thirsty football supporters. It seemed that the beer formed a critical part of warming up the vocal capacity before heading into the fortress. Screaming was the norm and discreet clapping not an option - another contrast to what I would experience the following day.

The teams ran out and the slow run-in from a famous leg-spinner was preceded by the sprints of an exciting winger called Shaun Wright-Phillips. I saw two men with blue jerseys shouting and screaming as if it was the best thing since sliced bread. They both had Chelsea shirts, one of which had "Mike" proudly printed on the back, and the other had "Mike's friend", Chelsea's version of Batman and Robin. Clearly their names were printed on the back in case they got lost or drunk beyond recognition. My roommate and I didn't know any of the songs but we sang as if we were part of the blue sea in front of us. At Lord's we weren't required to do any singing, only clapping. This allowed us to max out our vocal gauge at Stafford Bridge, as we weren't going to be needing it the next day.

I remember how these two days brought about questions around living a balanced life. I did not want to favour or lean towards any of the two supporter bases. I wanted to be able to relate to the fiery supporters of Stafford Bridge as well as the sophisticated folk of Lord's. I was pleasantly surprised by my revelation, only to find that the lessons learned from that weekend were not over yet.

When we arrived back home in London, I remember walking into our shared accommodation. My fellow house-mates consisted of a great bunch of friends, with the odd vagrant checking in for short bursts throughout the year. These men were usually in their late twenties or early thirties, and on this particular occasion two of them were sharing a room while their friend stayed on our living room couch.

This same friend had been released from prison only a few weeks prior to stumbling onto our couch. Each of them had a serious drug problem which landed them in jail on several occasions. I remember my foundations being rocked when I learned that they were all from South Africa, and initially arrived in London for the same reasons I did that year. They got stuck and ended up getting involved with the wrong crowd, which transformed a two-year travel experience into a foreign prison of addiction. The drug I saw them using the most was marijuana.

They had nothing in their lives that anyone could aspire to and used to sit in front of the television every night just to get high and pass out. I'm not judging - just saying what I realised I didn't want. This was a daily occurrence that illustrated their dependency and how they had completely lost their sense of purpose. If only they knew how much God loved them. There was no ambition, no hope for a family life, solid career, or even just pursuing something meaningful. I remember thinking to myself that I never wanted to be like that or in that situation.

They lived an unbalanced life and their existence became a poisonous routine that left us all speechless. They would usually start the evening by cooking a frozen pizza from the local supermarket. As soon as the pizza was in the oven, they would proceed to roll their joints for the evening. You can laugh at that, but only so much. All you could see was a cloud of smoke hovering above the living room, and three grown men, entering the prime of their lives, lounging at the edge of their chairs. They were totally oblivious to the reality of their situation. The sharp smell would penetrate the entire house.

The smell of the drugs and the food was bearable, but the smell of defeat not so much. Tired eyes were accompanied by a lifeless hand grasping the top of a stack of pornography DVDs next to them. Unlike the football fans of Chelsea or the cricket supporters at Lord's, I never wanted to be able to relate to these men. I knew that addiction, dependence and despair were not part of the future I wanted. This experience showed me how quickly it can happen. It was a vicious trap that men who came from my country fell into. Again, you need to learn this for yourself, because we get warned so often but it only sinks in when we see it for ourselves. I learned what I didn't want.

***

In 2006 I was visiting the beautiful city of Cardiff, the capital of Wales. Joining me on this adventure was my cousin and one of my friends. We'd booked out the weekend for what was to be a memorable occasion, an event which would later be shared on numerous family gatherings in the years to follow.

It is incredibly easy to visit different countries in Europe. Given their close geographical proximity, you can simply jump on a bus or a train and find yourself in a different country within a few hours. This is exactly what we did when we left England on an early Friday morning bus scheduled for a 06:00 am departure to Wales. I recall the bus tickets being dirt cheap, as we paid about each for a three-hour ride. On our way there, my cousin made a flattering yet cheeky comment about one of the ladies on the bus - in our native Afrikaans language, of course. You can only imagine our surprise when she turned around and gave him an unexpected reply in our mother tongue. Even though she appreciated the comments, she was not interested and basically got off at the next stop. Until this day, I'm not entirely convinced she had to; it might have been a desperate attempt to escape the unwanted attention. We were all a bit disappointed but immediately got over it as soon as we arrived in Cardiff.

My cousin ran into the shop opposite the bus station and bought as many alcoholic beverages as we could carry. We trekked to our local backpackers' for check-in shortly afterwards, almost leaving our bags behind in our desperation to carry the refreshments. The receptionist gave us our second dose of rejection as she kindly showed us the door for being there too early. Lucky I could handle it. We found ourselves in the streets of Cardiff next to the River Taff that flows through the centre of the city. The river was a spectacular reminder of where we were, with the Cardiff Castle proudly visible in the background. Whilst contemplating what to do with a bunch of luggage and two cases of beer and cider, we naturally deviated to a beautiful park located next to the Castle.

The Castle is surrounded by high walls and looks straight into the city. Bute Park, on the back left wing of the Castle, boasted beautiful trees, flowers, walkways, and three out-of-sorts South Africans. We graciously sat down on a nearby bench and started reaping our reward for carrying the refreshments. We could have easily been mistaken for homeless people. It didn't take long for our vocal chords to kick in and we started singing our own Afrikaans rap songs at the top of our lungs. There were pedestrians giving us stares from all over the place. It did not matter - the moment was too special. We had come a long way for Bute Park and we would deflect all judgement.

We eventually managed to check in and made our way to the local Walkabout. These pubs can be found across the world and are known as a great place for southern hemisphere travellers to get together and have a few beers. The interior of the pubs is usually a mixture of national South African, Australian and New Zealand colours. It does feel comforting in a way. I find that it was almost like sharing the experience with your friends and family even though they were not there. I have a lot of wonderful Walkabout memories and have been in a few of them during my travels. They never disappoint and I'm looking forward to visiting a few more in the future.

The next day we came across two Welshmen who found themselves in the middle of what you might call a southern hemisphere triangle. We were at the Walkabout again. The men had been visiting the capital from a small town about an hour or two away. We started talking and within minutes received an invite to go back to their hometown. Even though we were intrigued by the thought of exploring the unknown, we politely had to decline given the rotten conversation up to that point. These men were not good news and they made me realise what I didn't want to be like when I got to their age.

My mind was riddled with the nostalgia of a pretty heavy hangover, but I managed to clear the fog and see something very contradictory to the beauty of Wales. The men were probably just over forty years old. Both were married with children and yet they were a long way from their families, both in body and spirit. They kept telling us how important it was to sleep with as many women as possible. Being the hopeless romantic that I am, I sat there thinking how sad and lost these men were. They had no maturity, no pearls of wisdom, no valuable insight, encouragement, dreams or ambition. It was a sad sight that showed what could happen to a man who did not get his priorities straight. This is not a self-proclamation of righteousness. I have been where they are. However, this is a chapter about realising what you don't want and how important it is to figure it out before it is too late. Can travelling help us to avoid pitfalls and get our house in order? I believe so. It makes you realise what you don't want.

The next morning, we booked a trip to the iconic Millennium Stadium, a true fortress that is well known across the rugby world. It was also the first rugby stadium capable of closing its roof whilst a match was being played. The stadium was designed for the 1999 Rugby World Cup which was hosted in Wales, which meant that it had been seven years since its launch. I was twelve years old at the time. I remember walking through the players' tunnel as part of the stadium tour which they combined with a sound clip of a cheering Welsh crowd, a moment I will never forget.

We were fortunate to have a lovely tour guide who was passionate about the sport and his team. He told us a story in which he referred to a specific championship match where Wales faced their old foe, England. The story was about the historical rivalry at the newly built stadium, which was at full capacity. At the time, the Welsh team had been going through a rough patch, yet the locals were hopeful for a victory. In the dying minutes of the game Wales were behind on the scoreboard, but only just, and a three-point penalty could take them to victory. The penalty got awarded on the halfway line with the distance to the poles posing a stretch too far for the kicker. The capacity-filled stadium went dead quiet and apparently you could have heard a pin drop. The kicker lined it up and the country held its breath. The silence was broken by shouts of elation as the penalty was converted. At the back of that story, I couldn't help but imagine what a special trip that would have been for those two Welshmen and their families. Learn what you don't want.

Travelling and experiencing life-changing events makes an impact on you that will last forever. You cannot be the same person afterwards. It took me a long time to admit that these types of adventures changed me. Be careful not to neglect the small things whilst on the road. In my case it took one conversation with two drunks to make me realise what kind of a husband and father I would like to be one day. I didn't know it at the time, but the conversation turned out to be so significant that it stands out ten years after our Wales weekend, and five years into my marriage. Thank you, Wales, for the beautiful memories and for helping me learn what I don't want.

I encourage you to reflect on similar conversations you might have experienced in the past. Talk to the Lord and ask Him to open the curtain on long lost memories that could possibly remind you of important lessons you might have forgotten.

The contrasting and changing landscapes opened my heart to new revelations. The traditions at Lord's and the cheers of the Chelsea fans reminded me of the importance of balance. That weekend was a lens on the dangers of self-destruction and its consequences. The beauty of natural and historical landmarks in Cardiff opened my eyes to the things that ought to be most important. Be careful of the lies - they are not necessarily what you want or need. I can't tell you what they are. You need to discover them for yourself. Go ahead and learn what you don't want.

CHAPTER 9

TODAY IS A GIFT - THAT IS WHY IT IS CALLED THE PRESENT

I would like to start this chapter by thanking Master Oogway from Kung Fu Panda for the heading. A master in the great art of kung fu, he encourages us to live in the present and I couldn't agree more! I have found that through experiencing various spectacles in the world, our ability to live in the present is both cultivated and enhanced, making it easier to live for today when needed. Why? Because when standing in front of things like the Eiffel Tower, the Colosseum or the Sistine Chapel, you can't help but be in that moment. It is simply too big to discard or to succumb to distractions.

In 2013, I was on my way to one of the Seven Wonders of the World. We had booked a trip to the Victoria Falls located at the southern end of Africa. The falls stretch over the borders of Zimbabwe, Zambia and Botswana. Danielle and I managed to get stuck on a very small plane and were unable to get seats next to each other. To make matters worse, we were joined by a tourist group not too concerned about personal hygiene. The trip of a lifetime got off to a smelly start as I waved to Danielle from the back of the plane. It turns out that travel agencies have preference when it comes to seat selection, and on that plane they had been reserved by the anti-shower activist group months ago. The smell was too much to bear. In opposition to Master Oogway's rule, my mind wandered, using the flight as an opportunity to escape.

We had been waiting for this trip for ages and it was such a relief when we finally got on the plane to Zambia. From here we would take a short taxi ride to our hotel in Zimbabwe, crossing borders together for the second time in one day. Travelling can be expensive and it can take months or years to save for a trip. I think that this is part of the novelty and why people appreciate and embrace it so much. I had just finished my studies and recently started working. There was something very unique and special about travelling with someone you love. My love for Danielle and travelling were both packaged into one small smelly airplane. It was a dream come true. We had not done much travelling together up to that point, and I was in awe, completely swept up in the moment. I highly recommend that you do this with a spouse, family member or close friend. There is no better time than the present! Make the booking today.

As we approached the Zambian town of Livingstone, the Vic Falls became visible from the sky. Every single person on that plane got lost in the moment. The present adventure started to unfold in front of us as the pure magnitude of this extraordinary natural wonder was the centre of our bird's eye view. You could hear people gasping for air as the pilot gave us the perfect aerial shot whilst crossing over the Falls. It was either the view or the smell, but I could clearly hear the gasps. The sheer power of the water is unimaginable, and in that sight I received confirmation that we serve an incredible God.

As we landed and exited the plane the weird smell disappeared, and the air was filled with an African bush aroma as unique and wonderful as it sounds. We quickly realised that we were no longer on home soil and joined the foreigners' queue to enter Zambia. We joked about how the guy stamping the passports looked just like someone out of a Blood Diamond movie. We nervously made our way to the front for our check-in, clinging to our passports in anticipation of our next stamp. Not only did they check our passports but also our yellow fever vaccination papers. We felt organised as I confidently flipped out the yellow booklet.

We proceeded to move outside the airport gates and our driver greeted us with a friendly smile. My heart swelled with pride as he held up the Steenkamp surname board. I'm not used to having my name displayed like that; in fact, I'm usually the one holding the board. I was doing everything in my power to impress Danielle, and this was all prearranged. I had a big shiny engagement ring in my pocket which I had been carrying with me since we left Johannesburg. I thought that the Vic Falls would be a really cool place to ask the most important question to the most important person in my life: *Will you marry me?* Master Oogway would have been proud.

As it goes with these romantic gestures, timing is everything. I had no choice but to trust my Monkey Lion philosophy of allowing travelling and the adventure therein to provide me with the opportune moment to ask, and then to live happily ever after. Simple.

We got into the taxi supplied by our hotel and the driver took us through the Zambian and Zimbabwe border. Our stay would be on the Zimbabwean side of the natural wonder in a town called Vic Falls. Sounds about right. We crossed the border followed by a bridge where you could see a good part of the Falls and one of the most iconic bungee jumping platforms in the world. And no, I didn't jump. Asking the girl of my dreams to marry me was enough leaping for one day. Also, I couldn't afford it.

I have never lived in the moment more than I did that weekend. I simply had no choice. We arrived at the beautiful hotel and everything was going smoothly. I had prearranged a romantic dinner for two at the very top of the lodge. It was small and intimate, in a secluded area overlooking the African bush. In a desperate attempt to not give away the life-changing event which was about to unfold, I quietly whispered to the receptionist to confirm the plans. I wish we had thought of a signal before the trip. Too late. I was winking so much that I almost lost a future fiancée. The staff at the lodge were to form part of the master plan in more ways than I could ever have imagined.

Nervously, I insisted on grabbing a drink at the hotel bar and was starting to rehearse my speech. I felt the weight of the ring in my pocket increasing by the minute. It is still a constant reminder of the incredible moment. This is something you only want to do once in your life, and thanks to Leonardo Di Caprio, Richard Gere, Hugh Grant and other romantic comedy movie stars, it has to be perfect. You've seen the scenario play out in movies a million times and always wondered how your moment will happen. Will I say the right things? Will it be romantic? Will she be surprised? And of course, will she say yes? We sat down for dinner at around six o'clock and started our seven-course meal (another first). We grow up faster than we realise.

Then the magic kicked in and it illustrated how a moment can take over if you pay attention and remain in the present. Coincidentally, a choir walked up to our table and started singing a song in the famous African a cappella style. Their tune and rhythm were absolutely beautiful. The voices of our very own personal choir, the clear African sky and a table overlooking the watering hole centred in the middle of the lodge - these elements created the perfect framework for our engagement canvas. When we asked the choir what the name of the song was, they said something about lovers and that was my sign.

I told Danielle that I had to go to the toilet after the group left, but I was actually chasing after them in the pitch-black night sky. It seems dangerous when thinking about it now. It took me a while to get to them due to my lack of agility. I ambushed them and the horror on their faces showed their disbelief. I asked them to please come back and sing the song about the lovers, to which they reluctantly agreed. They realised it was safe and lowered the singing props, also known as spears, as we moved back to the table. I caught my breath and gave them the signal. Yes, we had a signal. It is never too late to redeem yourself, and I wish the receptionist was there to witness it.

God decided to send a herd of elephants at exactly that moment, and before I could sit and ready myself Danielle exploded with excitement as the majestic creatures arrived at the watering hole. The unbelievable thing is that the elephant is her favourite animal. We all stood there in the moment, witnessing these spectacular mammals going about their business. The moment could not have been more perfect, and as captivated as I was, I remembered my end of the bargain. The choir started their lovers-in-the-night tune and they did a beautiful job as expected. I got down on one knee and made a few promises with the Zimbabwean choir and the elephants as my witness.

She agreed to the terms and gave me a big fat yes. I hugged and kissed her and fell in love with her all over again. Looking to my right, I expected to see the choir crying just as much as we were, but they weren't. We got a slow clap and a few smiles before they left to romanticise the next group of visitors. I was elated and overwhelmed, completely overtaken by the moment. Master Oogway was right; that day was a gift.

I acknowledge the fact that this is an extreme example of the importance of staying in the moment. It is pretty easy when so much is at stake. However, I do feel that it demonstrates a couple of important points. It brings forth the question of whether we truly live in the moments of our lives, or whether we take them for granted. Society backs us into a corner where fear and anxiety often drive us toward future concerns or past regrets, delivering bags filled with complex envelopes of self-doubt and absent-mindedness. Fear is the number one obstacle to travelling - a negative mindset to avoid.

Today, the woman that I got down on one knee for in Zimbabwe is the same one making our morning coffee. She makes it without elephants, a watering hole or a choir. Just out of her own kindness, often before sunrise. But because we shared that moment, I tend to appreciate it so much more. Travelling is a source of shared experiences with no measurable monetary value. It binds people in a profound way. We can either complain about things that have not yet happened or have already happened, or we can take note of the actively beautiful things happening around us. Travel reminds me of the positive things in my life, and there is nothing that shakes my negative cage like a key that unlocks a new terrain to explore. The freedom that comes with travelling has made me a better person by giving me valuable insights as to why I need to keep working hard at appreciating the moment.

***

In 2010, I found myself in another African country west of Zimbabwe. It was three years before my romantic proposal. I was busy trekking through the African bush with a great friend and that was all that mattered at the time. People are stubborn and we often need to be forced into the moment. I'm guilty of this. Perhaps you can relate? We were driving down one of the main roads in Botswana and witnessed elephants walking next to it - incredible. It was like doing a game drive in a nature reserve, only it was on one of Botswana's main highways. These spectacular animals make you sit up straight, especially when our worlds intertwine so naturally, a sight which is almost impossible to find in a modern world. We were forced to be present and in the moment. Travelling can afford you such opportunities.

We made our way to the accommodation for the evening, a truly magical place called Elephant Sands. We set up camp and got ready for an evening of good company and laughter. We hung out and talked about life and everything in between. These conversations are priceless. Whilst sitting and sipping, we heard a slurp that I cannot describe. I looked over my friend's shoulder and saw an elephant drinking from the swimming pool! I was forced into that moment, as it hit me like a ton of bricks. What was I witnessing? Not far away from us you could see this graceful animal drinking from an unlikely watering hole - or according to the friendly staff, it was a very common sight and not so unlikely at all.

Botswana didn't stop there. It gave us another sense of its natural wonders when a pack of wild dogs came through the next morning. My friend came running to me like an injured gazelle. All I could see was dust and hand gestures which looked nothing like wild dogs. He indicated that they were at the "unlikely" watering hole. We ran towards the swimming pool like nine-year-old boys not worried about exams, life or other trivial things. We were forced into the moment. We left Elephant Sands shortly after, stunned by what this trip had delivered within the first few nights.

From there we made our way to Kasane, a town in the northern parts of Botswana, next to the Chobe River. Our adventure continued into an afternoon fishing session just after we witnessed a warthog at the local supermarket. The present delivered another gift as the famous African sun set over a river which sustains so much life. Master Oogway must be an African turtle.

The present had one more gift. We went out that evening and got picked up by a local taxi driver. I awkwardly made conversation as my trademark small talk kicked in. With his ears bleeding, he asked us whether we had seen a buffalo yet, and also if we knew that it was one of the most aggressive animals in Africa. No on both counts. He suddenly pulled up his hand brake and turned on the vehicle's headlights. The taxi ride turned into a rollercoaster. We were forced to stop and be in the moment, frightened and full of adrenaline pumping though our veins. There it was, a mighty buffalo staring us straight in the eyes. Then all of a sudden it was quiet. Gone were my chatter and my thoughts. I had no thoughts at all. The driver softly whispered that it was at this spot every night, grazing on the lush grass of the area. He also used the opportunity to advise us not to walk back, and to rather give him a call to complete the return trip. Fair enough. Once again, Africa had forced us to be in the moment - to be in the present.

Elephants are incredible creatures and many say that they are closer to humans than we think. They cry when something happens to their loved ones. They protect and defend their young fearlessly and with a relentless love. They are emotional animals. Why were they at the watering hole in Zimbabwe that night? At exactly that time? Being present back then affords me the luxury to reflect on the detail now. I'll never know, but perhaps I should use their characteristics and emotional capacity as a friendly reminder of the way in which I should cherish my beautiful wife: to treat her with the utmost respect and compassion and to meet her in the middle - at the watering hole - and to nurture someone so precious, who reflects love which originates from heaven. The Lord has never expressed His love to me more than on the day He decided to put Danielle in my life. I'm grateful for these moments of reflection. Thank you, travel. If you have experienced the privilege of travelling with a loved one, I know you have a similar story!

Remember to stay in the present. Try not to frighten people. And I would highly recommend a signal; always have a signal. Use the power of travelling to remind you of the important truths around staying in the present. It can so easily be forgotten. New terrain can help. The present is indeed a gift, just as Master Oogway promised. Make it count. Plan your trip today.

CHAPTER 10

ALONE IN THE DARK

Travelling can often be a daunting and scary endeavour, and I feel it is important to include in this book some examples of the challenges of being abroad. It is definitely not all flowers, unicorns and rainbows. The Ireland story in a previous chapter showed some of the challenges we inevitably face. It most certainly has its down moments and difficulties. Anyone who has ever been abroad will be able to relate to a moment of despair where they just wanted to go home. Venturing into the unknown is not easy and it comes with a collection of unique challenges and uncertainties. If not, then everyone would have done it. These moments are to be expected given the nature of the cause, but herein lies the opportunity for exceptional growth and self-development. One of the greatest gifts of travelling is learning more about what you are capable of handling, where your inner strength lies, and how you can tap into that strength as you face everyday life challenges.

It was 2006 and I had just got onto the London Underground tube from a suburban area called Leytonstone. The area was very well-known for its demographic, being made up of thousands of South Africans. You could see this in the wide selection of South African products available on the shelves of the local grocery stores. As mentioned before, London was the start of something beautiful but it came with many unexpected challenges. After settling in and finding a good job as a security officer, I ended up having a pretty hectic routine which started at 04:00 am every morning. Getting up in the cold took some real effort, particularly as winter started rolling in towards the end of the year. The experience was filled with darkness and took lots of discipline to maintain.

Getting on the first train to leave for work was non-negotiable. Anything less and you would be late, which is a massive problem if you are the guy with the keys to the building. I could spot the South African polar bears on the train, all characterised by the many layers of clothing to keep them warm. After all these years I am still able close my eyes and feel the rattling of the train as it moves through the underground tunnels, all dark, all the time.

I had to get off at a certain station and by God's grace managed to stay awake most days. However, some days I dozed off and would be late, having to catch a train in the opposite direction back to where I needed to jump off. From there I would start walking to work, cursing occasionally about my decision to voluntarily put myself through the agony. I would be upset at myself for falling asleep and having to now explain my whereabouts. The brisk walk doubled up as the only exercise for the day as well as a rude awakening to the responsibilities of being independent. The smells of coffee and bakeries were all around and I recall seeing a number of people lining up to get their daily caffeine fix.

I had mornings where I could smell the sweet aroma of independency, adventure and freshly baked croissants. But there were also mornings where there was not enough sun and I could smell the awful scent of urine next to the train station. I often felt cold, anxious, tired and irritated. I would continue walking in my security clothes. I was a proud professional security guard - or, as I liked to say, Double-O-Afro. I had a huge jacket and an MP3 player which allowed me to listen to all my favourite songs. I still get goosebumps when one of them gets played, immediately making a correlation to that daily routine walk.

I worked as a security guard in the heart of London in an area called Soho. This was the red-light district of London. As part of my security duties, I had to open the building at 06:00 am and close it again at 10:00 pm. This meant that I was working 16 hours a day (excluding Fridays, where I could leave early at 07:00 pm). This took place five days a week. I can't imagine how I took on those long hours and the boredom that came with it. Luckily, I had training in clock watching. This is obviously not the case for all security guards, but I wasn't great at my job. I worked at an English College for foreign students and my main duties included turning the alarm on and off, keeping the key to the vending machine safe (big mistake on their part) and checking students' cards before they were allowed to enter the building. It was very challenging and I struggled to keep up with the demands of staying awake and doing my duties whilst keeping a smile on my face.

But taking responsibility while grinding out the hours every day made me grow a lot as a person. Even though the College environment gave me a chance to interact with the students passing in and out, it became clear to me that when you work that many hours in a day your mind starts to switch off and you don't really engage as you should. Fortunately for me, I had an incredible friend named Ramos from Colombia, who was the only person in London I knew who had a credit card. This enabled me to buy an online membership to watch South African TV (KuduClub), which made a huge difference in helping me get through my day. Ramos was in charge of the cleaning team and naturally it meant that I got to see him every morning as I arrived to open the facilities. He was always smiling and often gave me valuable words of encouragement and wisdom. Most importantly, he had the ability to make me feel that I wasn't alone in the dark. He would phone me on the mornings where I had missed the train or fallen asleep en route, covering for me when I needed help. It meant so much to me - he was such a great friend.

We also had a British guy who came in once a month to check the plumbing, I can't remember his name, but he too made the pain more bearable. He could always make me laugh. I remember him asking one of the Caribbean women (who was part of the cleaning team) for a key one morning. She gracefully removed it from her bra strap and handed it over to him. This was a common pocket option in Africa so I wasn't surprised, but obviously not so common in England. He looked me straight in the eyes, took a massive sniff and gloated as if he had just won the lottery. He then proceeded swiftly to check the pipes, invigorated by his unique sense of adventure. It made his day, every time.

Along with my two friends, I also met three elderly ladies from the administration department. They were originally from Asia and had been living in England for many years prior to my arrival at the College. These ladies decided to adopt me as their long-lost son and they genuinely became like mothers to me. They always made sure I was okay, asking me whether I needed anything, and when I got sick they gave me a bag full of medicine. I learned that most people don't talk to security guards, or even greet them for that matter. But these few people decided to go out of their way to make me their friend. God sends the right people onto your path at exactly the right time. He knew that I needed some help and He made His presence known to me through Ramos, the plumber and the Asian Mum Society (AMS).

It is difficult to explain to someone how it feels to work such long hours whilst also being in an incredibly isolated environment. I'm sure there are many people with worse stories about their jobs, but for me this wasn't an easy thing to endure. It was hard.

As briefly mentioned, I was not very competent at my job or suited for it. I was a small and chubby guy who hated fighting or any form of confrontation. I had never thrown a punch, and with my infamous afro looked more like a clown than a crime fighter. I often went to the bathroom to sleep on the toilet, not because I'm a lazy person, but simply because my body just could not take the long hours. I also remember having to occasionally ask a group of what looked like Russian body builders for their College passes - or I would not let them enter the building. What a joke. We all laughed; even I did. I felt alone in the dark on many occasions but the fact of the matter is that I wasn't. God was there with me. God is always there surrounding you with His angels. Ironically, you'll find Him and those that serve Him in the most unlikely of places.

So what do I take away from this, and why is it helping me today? Firstly, it makes my current eight-to-five job look like a little hill compared to the mountain of a sixteen-hour isolated double shift. Did I mention I had to go in on Sundays from time to time? It also made me understand the hardship that many people go through every day without having other alternative options. I never enter a building without greeting the security guard or access gate keeper. I try and make sure that I'm extra friendly to the cleaning staff when they enter my office or I bump into them around the office building. It taught me compassion and a whole lot of humility.

Today I can somewhat understand what some people go through every day, and I know how honourable the work is that they are doing. Those six months as Double-O-Afro taught me that I could endure a lot more than I could ever imagine and that I was never, really, alone in the dark. You might be able to relate, or the story might still need to be written for you. But hopefully you'll find out soon enough that there is much more to you than you can ever imagine. Your capability to go beyond what you perceive to be your threshold is only limited until it gets tested. Travelling is a good measuring stick.

***

It was 2011 and we had just reached base camp, on our way to row the Orange River. The plan was to cross the Namibian border from the north-western parts of South Africa, and to row for six days whilst sleeping next to the river, under the stars. This seemed like a very romantic and fairy tale-like idea, but to be honest it was another thorough learning curve. You need a particular personality to enjoy this kind of trip and I'm the first to admit that I wasn't ready for it. Ironically, I needed it more than I could ever imagine. As you know, I'm not the most athletically gifted individual and neither is Danielle - she's small and petite while I'm short and chubby. We quickly realised that rowing the Orange River wasn't intended for our specific skillsets. We enjoyed the rowing events on PlayStation when playing our Olympics game, but that was about it.

Nevertheless, we were there after a gruelling 25-hour drive, and it was time to go. The trip had started out poorly when my friend lost a wheel just outside a town with a population of about 25 people. It took a few trips with the towing service and a check-in at the local tyre shop before we finally made Namibia. Danielle picked up a ride with friends who formed part of the convoy, while I was tasked to keep the unlucky driver company as he searched for a tyre in the middle of nowhere. It set the tone for the trip.

Once at base camp, we were set to start the trip but instead of looking like an Olympic rowing team, our group probably gravitated more towards looking like a group of Alcoholics Anonymous escapees making a run for the border with loads of alcohol and no ice. How was the lack of ice situation not considered before getting onto the kayaks? Especially in that heat? Rowing into the desert landscape with no ice? The majority of the group were couples, including us, and this would not only prove to be a challenge both mentally and physically but also for all of our relationships. Danielle and I shared a two-seater kayak with limited space for our bags, food and drink supplies. Thank goodness for short legs.

One of our friends attended the trip on his own and was in charge of rowing the portable toilet. It was his rowing partner - silent but violent. No matter how physically or mentally tired I was, I just kept reminding myself that had this trip been two years earlier, I would have been the one rowing with the toilet. The trip included a few massive water rapids tailor-made for your typical adrenaline junkies. We came to a stop shortly before one of the main rapids on our itinerary, and the instructor strongly warned us that it was time to focus and pay attention. Danielle and I looked at each other with eyes like a deer, or a buffalo, in headlights. Two group members went before us and had a massive "cheers" with their beverages before going down the epic rapid. They fell over immediately and didn't die. We figured that this was a good sign for us. We did a great job in manoeuvring through the wild rapids of the Orange River and bought the photos after the trip to prove it.

The thing about this trip was that it took away all the creature comforts. We didn't have shade in the desert-type landscape, and as I said, the toilet was floating on a kayak. It just got warmer and warmer as temperatures rose, with nowhere to hide. I wasn't myself that trip. I struggled with a lot of things, but being there with Danielle in Namibia forced me to reassess things. I remember picking a fight with one of my friends, which is not like me at all. I knew I had to do some serious soul searching and press the reset button in my life. The trip forced me into the reserves of my inner strength, making me aware of the situation I was in and who I wanted to be going forward. Lying there alone in the dark after walking away from a petty dispute over drink mongering, I realised that something inside me was longing for a change. There was a dim light inside my own darkness.

When travelling, there are these moments that tend to grasp you and stick with you. On the fourth night of the trip, my body hit a wall; all the heat and rowing had taken its toll. God was pressing in and I was ready to listen. We were sleeping on a blow-up mattress and I remember getting sick while lying next to Danielle. I felt she deserved a lot better and I knew in that moment that I did not want to be this person anymore. I felt uncomfortably overweight, unhealthy, unproductive and not very ambitious. I was worried and felt lost. My time had come to re-commit my life to my faith and to place Jesus at the centre, which was something I had lost over the years.

I believe that these challenges found within our adventures orchestrate important moments of reflection. When out of our comfort zone, it often brings forth an opportunity for you to experience His divine intervention, a moment of clarity which had been blocked by being in a complex and robust society. These truths can only be found in unknown and uncharted territories. Experiencing the grace of absolute clarity and hence the repentance born out of that moment is critical in order to move forward in your life. Sometimes you simply have to let go of the old in order to experience the joy of the next phase in your life. It takes inner strength to accept and acknowledge, and to make a difficult decision. The path to paradise often starts at the gates of hell, unfortunately. Was the harshness of the desert a coincidence? I don't think so.

I woke up with the same determination the next morning, as if someone had turned a page on my behalf. I simply knew that it was time to move forward, and I made the decision that I wanted to refocus my priorities. I remember sitting with Danielle under the late afternoon shadow which reflected off a cliff next to the beautiful flowing Orange River. The sun was setting and the earth cooling down after another extremely hot day. We made a few promises to each other which would turn out to be the foundations of our marriage and relationship going forward. The challenge gave us new hope and made us realise that as a unit we have the inner strength we need to row like Olympians.

I had felt alone in the dark the night before, but woke up to a sunrise with one of God's angels. It turned out to be an incredible trip at exactly the right time, and despite some hardship it is something I would recommend. The Namibian desert landscape worked its magic and gave me some fresh perspective. Today I look back and remind myself of the promises we made there, not in the dark but at dusk.

***

In 2019 I found myself in magical Brazil, a place with a uniquely festive atmosphere and island-like lifestyle. It was a country with a vibe I had never experienced before. My time in Brazil is well documented in one of the later chapters, so for the purpose of the current concept, I will highlight a single experience we had in Paraty, the focus being on how difficult challenges can bring people together when collectively faced whilst travelling.

By this stage Danielle and I had been married for four years. We had booked a three-week trip and our third stop on the itinerary was a small coastal town called Paraty. When we arrived at the destination, I started feeling ill and was trying to supress the symptoms as I didn't want to place a damper on this magical trip.

Travelling is the best possible thing you can do for your relationship with your spouse or partner. Sharing unique experiences brings you so much closer to each other and creates a bond which cannot be articulated - or broken, for that matter. But make sure that you choose wisely around who to take with you when planning your next trip, because on the other end of the scale, challenges faced while travelling can also force people apart.

On the first night in Paraty, I found myself lying in bed, alone in the dark once again, thinking how to approach the situation. I was a bit concerned and wasn't sure how to break the news or even what to do. We didn't know anything about the medical infrastructure in the small coastal town or who to reach out to. I told Danielle that I was ill and needed some medicine to help me get through the illness as quickly as possible. I was worrying that I might run the risk of being sick for the rest of the trip, with Rio De Janeiro still ahead. Instead of fighting, we were drawn closer together, and we immediately made plans on how to best handle the situation. Before I knew it my wife was leading the way to the nearest hospital. I would love to say that I was macho enough to decline, but I couldn't wait to see a doctor - even if we had to communicate via Google translate.

We sat hand-in-hand in the reception area whilst waiting for our number to be read out in Portuguese. As soon as we arrived, we had been given a ticket and taken a seat in the dilapidated hospital. That was daunting and it became a serious challenge rather quickly. No one wants this while on a trip but we had to make it work. We waited for at least an hour. It felt dark once again.

But when my number was finally called, in typical Brazilian fashion, we were treated with nothing but love and kindness. A wonderful doctor did a routine check and prescribed some medicine. If only I'd had this in Ireland. We were off in no time and didn't even have to pay for the medicine. Challenge accepted and conquered. It was off to the hotel for some free Wi-Fi and recovery time.

I hope that these stories will help you realise that things will never be perfect when travelling. But that is no excuse not to do it. Don't let the fear stop you. The Monkey Lion analogy is about transforming the fear of travelling to embracing the unknown. Even the bad stuff turns out to be good - you'll see.

There will always be some sort of challenge, and that is all part of the adventure. These challenges will make you stronger and will become less daunting the more you travel. Do not fear the challenges or the dark moments. They will come and you will be more than capable of handling them. Remember that you are never truly alone in the dark.

CHAPTER 11

WHAT ARE YOU PUTTING IN YOUR BODY?

Figuring out what works best for you in order to be physically, mentally and spiritually happy is key. Travelling has the ability to speed up the self-awareness process and the discovery of your preferred lifestyle. It is important to gain ideas and opinions from around the world to help you shape your own unique philosophy. I would recommend venturing into the unknown to discover the different methods and means of living, and to diarise your own transformational travelling in a Monkey Lion journal. Write down your travel stories. They matter immensely and will most likely assist you in gathering insight into how you want to live your life.

In 2006, a few of my colleagues and I were on a lunch break at the Barracuda Pub in London. We made a quick stop at the local supermarket and I bought the bargain of a lifetime: a two-for-one hamburger special. The yellow label with the marked down price was enough to convince me that I was making a choice that would most certainly be in my best interest. I walked back to work with a rumbling tummy and the exciting prospect of eating for two people.

I remember sitting down and opening my pack of burgers and getting a look of sheer disbelief from one of the Polish girls who worked with us. It was a look of absolute disgust as she loudly announced her disapproval. The words "what are you putting in your body?" still cut through me like a sharp knife. It was in broken English but I still felt it. I recall being extremely embarrassed and at a complete loss for words. The logical response was to simply laugh it off and keep on eating. Coward. This moment confirmed my self-diagnosis of being a nervous eater. Whether she knows it or not, those words have stuck with me until this day. I only later realised the importance of looking after your body. Even though I was obviously not practising self-awareness back then, it was enough to give me my first taste of its importance.

It is interesting that my journey around the essentialness of cohering body, mind and spirit began while I was holding two cheeseburgers in a pub. I wish someone had said something earlier and also much more directly. You simply cannot be fully happy and at peace if you keep on pressing the self-destruct button. I know this truth only because I have been there. It took me a year in London to realise how much I had stopped caring. It was brutal. Letting go of your physical wellbeing can be damaging in more ways than one. It also affects other areas like the mind and spirit. Physical wellbeing lays the foundation for the other two components, and eventually it became the first step in my healing process. Perhaps you needed to hear that today? The question is a place to start your journey. What are you putting in your body?

***

Later on in 2006, I had a similar experience in Germany. I found myself in a small student town called Heidelberg, a place notably characterised by a beautiful castle, river and cheap champagne. We were approaching the end of our European tour and I was strapped for cash, a theme throughout 2006. Heidelberg hoisted another red flag of how I was neglecting my physical wellbeing. We were gliding through the streets after playing hide-and-seek at the Heidelberg Castle up the hill. We made our way back down and I was extremely thirsty from walking and pulling up my oversized pants. I saw an inviting chalkboard sign saying that champagne was being sold at 1€ per glass. That's 1€ a glass: are you kidding me? I had to investigate. I was convinced that the castle trip would be followed by my knight in shining armour, which turned out to be a neatly dressed German lady. She was a salesman and I was a fool. *Prost*.

I bought and drank as much as I could and wobbled back to our German accommodation fully ready and committed for the after party. Unfortunately, the price was more than I could bear. I now had to deal with an empty wallet and an upset stomach. My negligence had taken a sadistic turn and I was made to suffer for it. It was inevitable after months of complete disregard for my physical wellbeing.

I returned to the sheds to find early respite, in the hope that I would be able to fight another day. The cheap champagne had me floored while everyone else was gulping German beer at the nearby pub. I was flat on my back, and with one last pull-up of my oversized pants, I went to sleep. It was rough. I made it through the night only to find that my fellow roommates had bailed on me. They too were looking for refuge. The snoring and moaning turned out to be a bridge too far. It was a low point, to be honest. It was a rare moment where I asked questions like: What was I doing? Why am I here? What was I putting in my body?

One of the essential lessons that travelling gave me was the importance of looking after your body. Self-love is not a fad. On my travels I had met many beautiful people with wonderful ideologies and perspectives. The ones that stood out were those who had a respect for self. They all had the foundations of self-awareness deeply engraved into their belief system, which rebelled against the lie of consumption-equals-joy. We get told that the more you have and use, the better and happier you will be. I prefer to focus on the balance between physical, mental and spiritual wellbeing, which should result in mindfulness. Travelling can open these doors and, more importantly, mirrors. What are you putting in your body? Is it cardboard cheeseburgers? Or cheap champagne?

***

It was 2008 and I found myself in the Land Down Under, beautiful Australia. It was a delightful sunny day and there was no reason to feel anything but good about life. At the time I had just started exercising again and had luckily brought my running shoes on the trip. They were really good quality shoes and were a legitimate option to sell if I ran out of money. The South African rand exchange rate wasn't good that year and I had already taken my study loan for the flight tickets. That left me with my expensive running shoes and my body to sell if things went badly. However, selling my body would most certainly lead to me having to pay the customer rather than the other way around. It wasn't an option. This left me with the shoes and, by God's grace, a really good Australian friend who looked after me.

I strapped on my savings plan and went for a run. This is such a spectacular way to explore and discover a place. I would highly recommend it for any traveller. I love doing regular things that one would typically do as a citizen. Things like running or walking, taking public transport, shopping at the local supermarket, picnicking in the park, driving, watching local TV shows, and so on. In this instance I was running in the streets of Melbourne, and I clearly remember my mind cleansing and filtering things. I needed to make sense of a lot of the emotions I felt at the time. Apparently, this is called processing, and it is important to mental wellbeing. I was discovering that the running was helping me get rid of everything that I needed to get out of my head, one stride at a time. It slowly helped me form the realisation around the next important lesson about self-love. Mindfulness. Travelling opened this pathway even though I wasn't there yet.

I kept running until a came to a road crossing which led to a park. The parks in Australia are incredible. They are beautifully maintained and offer residents a wonderful opportunity to enjoy different kinds of exercise. Whether it is using the public stationary gym equipment, riding on cycling roads, or simply running or walking. Usually when someone runs in South Africa there is a good chance that the person is being chased. Not in Melbourne, not in Australia. It was the one place I could see myself living forever.

I ran for about thirty minutes before reaching one of these beautiful parks. I sat down on a nearby bench to catch my breath. I took a moment and it felt as if everything just went dead quiet. While on that bench, I had my first real conversation with God for many years. I can't fully explain it, but I needed to be there to realise that He was with me - always. It was overwhelming to think that no matter where you are in the world, God is there with you. I learned that His presence is not limited to or bound by your location, but that He is omnipresent all the time.

My lungs were filled with air and this combined perfectly with the quiet surroundings. I had the opportunity to be mindful. The cheeseburgers of London were replaced with the fresh air of Melbourne. I took a moment to think about what I was putting in my body. What I was doing for my mental and spiritual wellbeing.

I found a clear link between mental, spiritual and physical health on that trip. I think it had a lot to do with the lifestyle of the Australian people that I met. They taught me so much without knowing it. They loved sport and being active, and the government created opportunities for them to pursue this lifestyle. A massive breakthrough in my life had been created by an opportunity that could only present itself through travelling and exploring. I was putting breath in my body and finally noticing the difference it was making to my mental health, the nourishing resources that it could provide. What is the ingredient for yours? It's different for all of us. Most importantly, where will you go to find it?

Mentally I felt strong, and this became a new lifestyle which I took back to South Africa. It came into fruition at the Orange River. Remember that the travelling Monkey Lion analogy is all about transformation. Transformation takes time. The discovery of mental wellbeing was taking shape. It is still ongoing, but at least it had been kicked into gear.

But God wasn't done with me just yet. On that trip another element was revealed. The final element of the tripod - spiritual wellbeing. It was more evident that day than ever before. It all came together. I was afraid and I felt vulnerable. I needed some help and guidance. I needed God's presence. I received a wonderful sense of peace that afternoon and I remember realising how big and wonderful He is.

Whether you are reading this book from the comfort of your home or while on holiday and travelling (even better), I would like to encourage you to take a moment and close your eyes. Just realise that He is there. He knows the battles and the challenges that you are facing in your life. He wants you to know that He is the same every day and that He is all you need. Take a moment and feel how much He loves you.

Be mindful of God's presence in your life. God is everywhere and in all corners of the world. Omnipresent. He was there with me in Melbourne. I needed Him to be and He showed up powerfully. I firmly believe that our peace of mind and spiritual wellbeing lie with Him, the Creator of heaven and earth. He loves you.

I needed to move as far away from home as I possibly could to discover these truths. Physical, mental and spiritual wellbeing goes hand-in-hand with faith. I was a student with no money, and took a huge leap of faith in 2008. When it felt as if the walls were coming down, He was there as always. He is there with you now.

I encourage you to travel in order to discover what a healthy balance looks like for you. The reality is that it is different for everyone. It does not need to include running or cheeseburgers. The common principle is that it gets revealed in unfamiliar and vulnerable spaces. Start making your plans and book an adventure. Why not add a fun activity or set a fitness goal? The air might just do you good. Perhaps you would be keen on a music gig in Nashville? If that is not your thing, then book a trip to the Vatican City and celebrate the arts. Alternatively, look at booking tickets to a few shows at local theatres in Buenos Aires. Be cautious of what you put in your body - physically, mentally and spiritually.

CHAPTER 12

PEOPLE MAKE THE PLACE

No matter where you are in the world, it is important to remember that the people make the place. In my adventures I have seen this time and time again. It does not matter how spectacular a place is, you need to be there with the right people. I have been incredibly fortunate in this regard, as my travels have always been filled with amazing people. The opportunity to share the experience of embracing new cultures and learning new things about yourself is priceless. You also get to reflect with people you travel with, and a bond is formed which can rarely be matched by any other collective experience.

I want to encourage you to not only make time and effort to see the world but to also invite your spouse, family or friends to join you on these adventures. From the initial planning phase, right up until when the plane lands back home, it is all much better when shared. I have learned that lifelong friends can be made on buses, trains and ferries.

Then there is the unique bond with new acquaintances that is created whilst travelling, through the short but impactful encounters.

It was 2016 and we were off to the beautiful landscape of Lesotho, a country located in the centre of South Africa. It has such a bizarre geographical location. I cannot imagine that there could be any other country like it anywhere else in the world. Perhaps the Vatican City? It is sort of the same thing, but then, not really at all. Lesotho certainly doesn't have a Pope, only a King. It is a country known for its beautiful mountains and one of the only places in Southern Africa that produces snow. There are resorts in Lesotho that get booked out a year in advance by people who enjoy the snow, skiing, high altitude and hot chocolate.

On the first day of our short trip, we jumped into my friend's car, ready to take on the intimidating Sani Pass, a monstrous mountain pass notorious for its steep elevation of 2876m. You cannot get up the Sani Pass or drive through the border of Lesotho with any sort of vehicle. It has to be robust and elevated, a machine with power and very reliable brakes. I cannot emphasise that last bit enough. You need to have the right means of transport to be allowed to make the attempt, or alternatively catch a lift with one of the tour operators. There are a few people who run or bike up the Sani Pass, but we weren't too keen on taking on that test of endurance.

My friend handled the steep climb like an absolute professional. Confidence was definitely not a problem. As one progresses, the steep mountain pass starts to show off its wondrous frozen lakes and waterfalls. It looked like a majestic ice palace with frozen elements lighting up the path all the way to the mountain top. We were taking photos and having a good laugh as we embarked on a once-in-a-lifetime road trip. With slow and steady caution and precision, we were forming our own ice-sculpture-like memories which would be frozen in time forever, together. Two couples taking part in one adventure with a shared love for travelling. In this case, it was African trekking and all its unique intricacies.

This was alongside the same friend who had taken me on as a brother in the African safari adventures mentioned in the previous chapters. We both have the longing to travel deeply entrenched in our blood, and live for these kinds of adventures. He is also the one friend who has always been the most honest with me. He has never been afraid to call me out, and that is something I truly appreciate. He is one of those people who make the place.

We continued to venture up the path and eventually made it across the border safely. We found our pot of gold when we stumbled upon the highest pub in Africa. We celebrated the night away, contemplating his driving skills and the fact that we actually managed to get our wives there in one piece. The shared love for travelling was officially extended. We were blessed with the opportunity to share this with our spouses. We were now able to make new memories collectively.

That night we drove from the venue to our accommodation at around midnight and it turned out to be even more frightening than the drive up. We had no street lights to guide us and I recall our female companions shouting worryingly in their high-pitched voices from the backseats.

I think we rolled the vehicle's wheels over a few traitorous rocks - I think. As we arrived at the low-cost accommodation, there was very little separating us from the other residents in the shared house. We could hear every single conversation from our fellow travellers and giggled nervously as we heard laughter turn into aggressive arguments. It felt a bit like the start of a horror movie but at least we were all in it together.

We didn't get much sleep that night with loud noises, intense arguments and a crisp cold breeze dominating the early hours of the morning. We woke up with empathy for our fellow troops and for the vehicle that did such a splendid job of handling the terrain. I remember seeing miles of snow which had fallen during the night, and feeling a great sense of peace as the snow carpet met with the African sunrise. I never thought that there would be a day where I would see snow in Africa. We carried on playing in the snow like small children. There are a few classic photos of us four which I can't wait to show my friends' baby boy who will be born in a few months' time. Lesotho was exceeding all expectations that weekend, but what made it really special was the wonderful people that I got to share it with.

The trip was planned at short notice and included a brief but intense drive. Lesotho was an impulsive decision that made me appreciate the people I got to spend it with. You need to make plans and set the budget. It doesn't have to be expensive. If you're young and single, get a few friends to join you or ask a family member. Alternatively, set a date with the couple you and your partner are close friends with, and arrange a weekend away in another country or state.

The opportunities are endless and the internet will give you plenty of suggestions. A travel experience can be simple, yet enriching like nothing else. Old friends become closer and history between people starts to evolve into folklore for generations to come. Invite the right people and they will surely make the place.

***

In 2006 we found ourselves in the capital of Italy. The great city of Rome is a place which hosts incredible magic and intricacy, especially given its legendary stories of gladiators, the Colosseum, iconic governments and ruling authorities. Ironically, Rome turned out to be one of the best places I have ever visited, but not because of the myths and the movies. It was fantastic because of the incredible people that I found myself with at the time. This was the European trip that helped me form special relationships in a short space of time. The lifelong friendships made in two weeks are simply irreplaceable. This is something you need to experience for yourself.

As our tour operator entered the Rome accommodation site, I went to a nearby pay phone to call my father. I finally had a chance to give him a quick phone call for a much-needed catch-up. It was so surreal being able to phone him from Italy and share that moment with him. How does a 19-year-old boy explain to his father that he is currently in Rome and just got back from visiting the Colosseum? The simple answer is that you can't explain it! I tried to fit in as much as I could during our 15-minute conversation. When I was growing up, I never imagined that I would be able to experience the things that I was experiencing in that moment. I felt really proud to be able to make that call. The adventure of travelling gave me a new sense of confidence and innocent bliss.

That evening turned out to be very different from gladiator battles, as we were instructed to join the group for a toga party. We were asked to get dressed in the items given to us, which were not very warrior-like at all. We didn't get any swords or armour, only leaves to use as a crown, and one blanket to cover our bodies. It could have been worse. At least we weren't having an Adam and Eve party with only the leaves - Italy would not be able to recover from that! I got to share this embarrassing moment with incredible people. People who made the place.

It was the closest I had ever been to looking like a Roman empress. We all sat around a long table making jokes and enjoying the wine, acting like kings and queens of the empire. We also watched a Springbok rugby match on the big screen, and myself and all the other South Africans busted out in song and proudly sang the national anthem. There was something wrong with our timing and we managed to finish the anthem halfway through the "actual" anthem on the television. This all transpired in front of a packed house full of foreign travellers. We didn't do our fellow South Africans any favours that day.

No problem, though, as I reminded myself that it was about the people and not the singing. We carried on through the night, until the security guard politely came to ask us to leave for our tents. I recall standing in the middle of the group doing the New Zealand Haka (New Zealand's traditional war cry) with my newly acquired Kiwi friend. Can you imagine the picture of two men dressed like Roman empresses shouting the Haka in their long white blankets? I don't think we did New Zealanders any favours either.

After we were asked to leave the area, another new friend and I were dying of hunger. Singing and dancing does work up an appetite. I'm pretty sure that Caesar had grapes after an eventful night in the palace. We quietly sneaked away to the tour guide tent, rounding our backs with a slight crouch. This was where they kept all the food for the tour. We managed to stumble across a vine of muesli bars. Italy is very well known for its cuisine and I can confirm that this was the best muesli bar I had ever eaten. However, I have a suspicious feeling that it was the new friend that I was sharing it with, and not the muesli bar, that made it taste so damn good. The people definitely made the place.

***

In 2006, I was on a plane with a very good friend, on our way to visit the country of Scotland. We had decided to take some time off and were on our way to Edinburgh for the weekend. Edinburgh had a magical feeling about it with a medieval atmosphere bolstered with the majestic story-telling features of a time so often portrayed in movies. Knights, queens, castles, battlefields, etc. The Edinburgh Castle is firmly imprinted in my mind as it made quite an impact on me. Seeing the statues of Robert the Bruce and William Wallace made it incredibly special. I love the movie *Braveheart* and have always been fascinated with the story of William Wallace's life. When I saw his statue with my own eyes, I felt closer to his legacy than ever before.

Being able to share that weekend and its experiences with my friend, along with a whole bunch of awesome people we met, made it exceptional. This story is about the acquaintances we meet whilst travelling. People you will probably never see again. You might become Facebook friends but that's about it. We visited the city during Halloween, which coincidentally matched the surroundings with that medieval feel. The local backpackers' where we stayed took us on a walking tour through Edinburgh and arranged a Halloween dress-up party that evening.

The wind that weekend was constantly blowing and had a very cold chill. Part of our tour included a stop at the graveyard and I remember that the tour guide mentioned how difficult it was to face the cold in a kilt. He also confidently claimed that he had no underpants underneath his kilt, which my friend and I agreed was the scariest thing we faced during our Scottish trip. The tour was really nice, though, and we had a good laugh while getting to know our fellow backpacker roommates. Hostels are the breeding ground for meeting new people, and are so effective in that way.

That evening we all dressed up in our Halloween outfits, making a colourful group consisting of a few interesting costumes. I remember guys like Texas Tom, who dressed up in a cowboy outfit, and Toilet Man, a guy wrapped in toilet paper. Toilet Man was an alibi for a French guy who could barely speak a word of English. He obviously had to make do with what was available at the accommodation. Thank goodness my German stomach bug was long gone. He somehow managed to wrap himself in all the toilet paper he could find. The tour guide remarked that no one was allowed to smoke near Toilet Man - fair point. I was wearing a Shrek outfit, which was mistaken for Hulk by a very polite young lady. She was obviously trying to be nice as the rest had no doubt.

Our band of misfits and superheroes moved on with our itinerary and visited some really nice spots in the centre of town. We went to a place which had a large dance floor and hosted a huge crowd. I remember dancing my heart out in between Texas Tom and Toilet Man, still in my Shrek suit. Now, that was scary. I'm pretty sure we must have been the most out-of-sync and disturbing boy band Scotland has ever seen. Once again the people made the place.

To my dismay I have not seen my lost boy band members since that evening. I wouldn't even be able to find them on social media because I never got their real names. They will always be Texas Tom and Toilet Man to me, and that is awesome. Every single one of the stories in this book can be linked to new acquaintances or once-off friends with whom I had an incredible experience at a certain place and at a certain time. I didn't always get their names but they were significant enough to be in this book. They made an impact on me and I'll never forget them.

We walked through iconic landmarks and landscapes. It was all so beautiful and Edinburgh will always be a special place to me. I remember the tunes of bagpipes loudly blowing through the main areas. It gives me goosebumps just thinking about the magnitude of being in the midst of such rich tradition and culture. Above everything else, though, it truly was the people that made the place that weekend.

The day-to-day challenges of everyday life can be daunting. They can often have a negative impact on our thoughts. We tend to lose sight of what is important. People are important. Shared memories are important. Reflecting on things with others can certainly help, whether it's old friends, new friends or acquaintances. The people or the memory can help you get through your current situation. These relationships carry us through trying times. Travelling can help you connect with people like nothing else.

Be one of the people that make the place. There are numerous platforms in various stages of your life where you can be that person. Focus on being an awesome father, mother, husband, wife, friend or colleague. The problem comes in when we rely on our circumstances or outcome to provide us with joy and happiness. Ultimately it is the people and our faith or inner peace that take care of the matter.

This peace through and with other people can only be achieved by focusing on God and asking Him to guide you to become a light to others. It is only through His Holy Spirit that we get the courage and conviction in our hearts and minds to prioritise others above our own needs. Making a difference in the lives of other people by truly adding value to them is what life is all about. The great thing about travelling is that it gives you a perfect platform from which you can carry your light to others. The manner in which you handle other people in these moments allows you to represent so much.

There might also be a chance that your current situation has stolen the need in your heart to love people. Travelling might be the gateway you need to remind you of this truth. It forces you to. People make the place and travelling affords you the opportunity to be one of those people.

CHAPTER 13

PERSPECTIVE FROM THE TOP OF A CATHEDRAL

Cathedrals are historical landmarks found all over the world and are particularly abundant in Europe. St Paul's Cathedral in London is one that I vividly remember. The cathedral has breathtakingly beautiful views that provided me with a unique perspective of a city that gave me so much. Perspective is one of the greatest gifts that could be bestowed on any person, no matter where you are. Perspective is everything! Travelling provides new and often much needed perspective. C S Lewis said that the only thing that really matters in this world is our own state of mind. I couldn't agree more. Travelling can provide you with an expanded perspective that will likely alter your state of mind for the better. A case in point is the perspective you find from the top of a world-famous cathedral.

In 2015 I was on honeymoon in Thailand. The once-in-a-lifetime break away was infused by the magical sunsets of Phuket and the tranquillity of Koh Samui. I long for trips like this. For a Monkey Lion traveller they can open a gateway into a time without too much responsibility or complication. A time where you can just focus on the moment and the experience, seeking new perspective. These adventures are rare and special. Their scarcity intensifies the novelty when they do happen for you. The perspectives almost become more expansive the older you get.

Marriage was a whole new chapter for Danielle and me, and we needed some time together following the huge build-up to the wedding day. We scheduled an elephant ride at one of the local elephant parks in the Phuket area. The people of Thailand were so friendly and we found it incredibly easy to do stuff while we were there. The service was excellent and always on time. We didn't meet a single person who wasn't super helpful.

We were picked up by a driver from the elephant park and he immediately made us feel like we were in good company. We even joked around a bit about the obvious risks. He was unable to fully comprehend our concerns, because of his limited English. What he did understand, though, was that we were on our honeymoon. We conveyed this by showing him the rings and giving the thumbs-up. We were able to get the message across successfully. He had definitely seen it before.

We embarked on this beautiful adventure with our new friend, who picked up a few fellow travellers along the way. This is where I often embarrass Danielle as my small talk shenanigans kick in. At least we were on our honeymoon, which meant that we were not allowed to argue. As we arrived, we were introduced to our local tour guide, a petite Thai lady who was just as friendly as our driver. The first thing she showed us was how Thailand farmers were able to successfully plough rice with their unique traditional method, with water buffaloes as the engines operating the plough machines. They make use of these strong animals by letting them drag the equipment across the land, enabling them to work the ground to produce the best harvest. It was truly impressive to get up close with these beautiful animals. We even managed to catch a ride around the rice fields, which became a useful marital metaphor. Sometimes being dragged through the mud is what you need in order to get the best harvest. How's that for perspective? Not from a cathedral, but from a farm tool.

We then moved onto the elephants. Each of these majestic animals was used to take us for a ride through their home. Elephants are very sentimental to us after their guest appearance at the famous engagement weekend in Zimbabwe. These elephants were massive and yet so incredibly gentle. Each elephant had a trainer that lived with them in the area. All the trainers stayed in small treehouse-like homes which were nestled in the heart of the Thai jungle. Apparently, this is the best place to raise and train the animals. Trainers and their animals become inseparable. We can learn so much from nature and its calmness. These trainers were calm.

Looking at the treehouse homes as we passed through, I realised the beauty in their simplicity. How often do we get lost in the details? These elephant trainers - or let us call them elephant whisperers - lived in these treehouses amongst the elephants every day. What a life that must be. It gave me some much-needed perspective. I couldn't help but envy these guys for a moment. They were totally separated from the technologies of the world and lived such purposeful, peaceful and unique lives. They had far fewer distractions than we do, with no screens that could invade their space or devalue their human interactions. No distractions enticed them to purchase their way to happiness.

While riding, we were taking a bunch of photos and I eventually asked our elephant driver to turn around for one. He gave us the biggest smile we came across in Thailand. His eyes told a story of a content man living close to nature. It gave an even better perspective than the one from a cathedral all those years before. We got some new perspective from an elephant's back: we don't need things to make us happy. We need animals.

Remember the wonderful driver who joined us for the day? He was lurking in the background while we were doing elephant trekking, feeding the elephants, taking water buffalo rides and visiting the curio shop. This humble man dropped us off at the hotel and walked up to me to hand over a small gift. This gift was to congratulate us on getting married. It was a small handcrafted wooden elephant that he had bought for us at the curio shop, his way of saying congratulations. I was stunned by the generosity of this immaculate gesture from someone who I think had a lot less than most. That was when I got the perspective that I try and carry with me every day: the importance of humility.

This man did not know us at all and yet he took the time to buy us a small wood crafted elephant. It proudly stands in our home today and will be with us forever. It is our reminder of what a pure heart looks like. It is our reminder of the importance of humility. I gave this man a massive hug after receiving our gift. It was probably the longest minute of his life. He had no choice. Perspective truly is the greatest gift that can be bestowed upon us. That day a few things changed for me, and I'm grateful that travelling gave me that opportunity. I will always be humbled by that gesture. Whether on a farm tool or an elephant, the real perspective came from the palm of that man's hand.

***

In 2017 we decided to book a trip to our neighbouring country, Namibia, in the lower south-west corner of Africa. We specifically decided to stay in a small town called Henties Bay, which is any onshore fisherman's dream holiday destination. My father-in-law is a brilliantly gifted fisherman and he had been fishing these waters for years. He grew up in Walvis Bay, which is only a few kilometres away from our destination. The area had stunning views with a contrast in landscape that I had never seen before.

As we made our way towards the famous fishing spots, we had the rolling dunes of the desert on our right-hand side, and the waves of the south Atlantic Ocean breaking on our left. The surroundings were mostly untouched, with little to no human activity the more we made our way north. The sand had a glitter-like glow as it stretched as far as we could see. The barrenness was beautiful, and I loved being exposed to this environment. The solitude was impactful, with absolute silence accompanying the dry landscape. It was tangible and clear. The silence was only interrupted by my mother-in-law as she turned up Bryan Adams at my request. Danielle rolled her eyes as we continued the journey. I was psyching myself up for the fishing.

We visited some really magical places, including the famous Dune Seven, which is known as one of the highest sand dunes in the Southern Hemisphere. We also managed to visit Walvis Bay, another small fishermen's town inhabited by beautiful pink flamingos that graze in and around the harbour. The birds added their unique colours to the German-like architecture of the homes and hotels. A few kilometres south of Walvis Bay is the tourist town of Zwakopmund, a town mostly built around the early German settlements. Here we had a traditional German lunch at a local restaurant and walked around a square that felt more European than African. There is so much to see in this incredible part of the world. One thing that was glaringly obvious was the humility of the locals, especially in Henties Bay.

The humility and kindness of the local residents were abundantly clear. A plumber came out to fix our water pipe issues late one evening. It was definitely a situation you don't want when away with family, but he made it easier with his humble approach and patience. He was someone I wish

Toilet Man could have met. Shortly after his arrival, an old lady came to meet with us. She was our host, and her cheerful spirit certainly contributed to the morale. She explained how she had caught one of the largest galleon fish ever seen in the area. Not that humble after all! But if you could hear her tell the story, you would understand. Innocent bliss reigned once again.

The Bible speaks about Christians being the salt and the light of the world, referring to the importance of humbling yourself to serve others. Henties Bay actually has the salt mines and light houses to illustrate this teaching. I felt that the people there were a very true reflection of this valuable perspective. It reminded me of my friend in Thailand. I have a Dune Seven rock standing next to his wooden elephant, the pair of artefacts serving as a constant reminder of this valuable perspective dished up by my travels. Humility is the key ingredient to contentment.

Another perspective was added to the recipe of contentment. If humility was the main ingredient, then gratitude must be the spice. Gratitude struck me in Henties Bay as I stood next to the ocean one late afternoon. I had just cleaned the fish which we had caught for the day, and I felt grateful regardless of the smell. In fact, even more so considering the good haul. Cleaning fish was probably the main reason why I made the squad to Henties Bay. But that did not matter - I loved it. It turns out that I'm not that good at catching fish but extremely good at cleaning them.

I never thought that God would lead me onto that patch of beach and ocean. I never thought that I would be in the position that I was in, or how blessed I would be through these adventures. I am not sure what your hurts, fears or condemnations might look like, but I know that there is a Father in heaven who loves you regardless. That is something to be grateful for. He will look after you as He has looked after me. He loves us all equally. The Bible says that once you see the world through God's eyes, you have obtained true wisdom.

I would like to encourage you to make an effort to seek the adventure that God has placed in your heart. See the world. Travel as far and wide as you can; or simply make wooden swords and go for a walk with your sons. It does not have to be extravagant. Neither humility nor gratitude is.

Travelling makes the clock stand still for a brief moment. Who knows what perspective you might get? You cannot help but be grateful when you travel. Namibia and Thailand gave me a perspective which I needed to understand and comprehend. The humility and gratitude of the locals I found in these spectacular settings made me pause for a moment. Elephant rides and sunsets led to humility and gratitude. The cultural nuance we experienced was priceless. These were unique perspectives.

The perspective from the top of a cathedral, where it all started, led me to powerful truths - truths found on the back of an elephant and on the beaches of Namibia.

CHAPTER 14

SOUL SEARCHING AND G-STRING BIKINIS

O ne of the greatest gifts travellers can experience when digging their shoes into the dirt road is the subsequent mud removal exercise. It gives you a unique opportunity to rediscover who you really are. Brazil generously offered me this chance.

It was thirteen years since my travels had started. In a country where every single person either wears a G-string bikini or a Speedo as their beach attire, it became apparent that they did not care too much for the opinion of others. They embraced their bodies and effortlessly exuded confidence wherever they were. It was hard to tell where the confidence came from, but eventually you did not even notice the skimpy dress code. It became apparent that the minimal attire was convenient for swimming, tanning, exercising and shopping. The people had boldness that eventually became the means through which the dirt road of a cluttered mind could be addressed - not that I enjoy or even wear Speedos.

In 2019 I was running on a Brazilian island called Ilha Grande, a piece of paradise only accessible by boat. The island is remote and far removed from civilisation. It boasts incredible peaks, beautiful vegetation and a rare feeling of remoteness, with no motor vehicles allowed. The tropical beaches run full circle around the 360-degree mass and deliver you with a slap-in-the-face sea breeze like none other. The running brought me peace and calmness as it emptied a long laundry list of dirty propaganda, false expectations and fortified lies which had been constructed by the various polarised and secular views of the modern era. The Brazilian island people reminded me of a lifestyle which brought welcome relief. I found myself pleasantly surrounded by this newly discovered serenity as I soaked up paradise.

I made my way back to our hotel only to lock eyes with what is most precious. My wife Danielle was cuddled up in bed mastering the art of rediscovery through rest rather than endurance. She glanced at me with a familiar smile and I realised how lucky I was to have a partner who understood me.

I took several walks and runs on Ilha Grande and met some amazing people throughout the journey. We found a popular coffee spot staffed with friendly locals who later became friends. One morning I looked at the barista and wondered when last I took a moment to learn a barista's name back home. I remembered how much I used to love meeting new people.

We continued the adventure by jumping onto a speed boat that was built to race over these waters elegantly. It reached several spots throughout the day, among them being the crystal-clear waters of Lagoa Azul. We jumped off the boat as we indulged in a long overdue adventure. Cleansing my cluttered mind had made it possible to embrace the present.

I was unlikely to miss a moment whilst submerged with my snorkelling gear. I frantically moved my goggles around as the water flowed through the mask, correcting the breathing pipe while I was at it. I looked like a first-time swimmer as I nearly drowned with my lack of snorkelling coordination. I didn't mind it too much, as my thoughts were clear enough not to take offence. I avoided getting tangled up in the web of self-absorption, and at that stage might as well have gone Speedo shopping.

Danielle and I had one set of snorkelling gear, and at my next turn I took the chance to swim out a bit further. I heard a girl shouting at me and I assumed that it was in Portuguese. It was under water so it might also have been English. The bubbles came to a complete standstill and I had a moment to enjoy the underwater view. It lifted like a curtain in front of my mask. I heard a second shout from the young lady and realised that it was the word "turtle", which is not Portuguese. My eyes lit up as if I had only just realised that I was actually snorkelling in South America.

I immediately attempted to go towards the direction in which the turtle alarm was sounded, with a swimming style that was something between and breaststroke and a stroke. Nevertheless, I swam the distance through perseverance and there it was in all its glory, an actual sea turtle gently cruising through the blue water of this spectacular underwater world. I looked towards my new sea turtle friend and she gave me the thumbs up. I followed the animal enthusiastically as it gently moved into deeper water. We swam next to each other for about ten minutes before it left me for the open waters. I swam back and maturely did several underwater fist pumps. The last time I had done a fist pump, I was thirteen. There was no more clutter, just pure joy.

On the boat, we made our way back to the main port and I could not stop feeling like a million bucks. The sea turtle experience was one of the all-time best moments of my life and one that belongs in the highlights reel of my existence. It also gave me some more credibility when claiming my island birthright and the certainty that nature was telling me to stay. I had it all figured out. We were going to stay in Brazil forever.

Danielle and I went to the Kebab Lounge that evening and met up with a new friend. It was his second night working at the restaurant and we bonded over his excellent English capabilities. He had an afro, which immediately drew me to him for obvious reasons. He forgot to take our order for the second evening in a row but it did not matter. It was all okay because the dirt road plagued with problems had disappeared in the cleaning process forced upon me by the island. The new insight reminded me of who I really am and what I enjoy.

These are heartfelt moments. Life changing. That moment provided me with the clarity that there were much worse things that could happen in life than I often think or worry about. I recognised how short my fuse had been over the last several months back home. I felt guilty and gave Danielle and our new friend a weird group hug. I made him take a photo with me so I could remember him for the rest of my life. I love these characters. Again, I considered buying a Speedo. Who cares?

A few days later, we took a minibus to Paraty, a culturally historic town in Brazil. A long overdue moment finally occurred when I grabbed a SUP board and achieved a goal set when I started my "one year without beer" challenge three months prior. Travel brings transformation. I had made a list of all the things I wanted to experience whilst fully committing to sobriety.

My first SUP ride was top of the list. I was able to be fully present, and enjoyed the moment partly because of the sobriety commitment, but also because my head was clear. The travel bug had kept sweeping the dirt off my subconscious mind. I looked towards the ocean and saw beautiful pockets of islands situated all around. I looked back and saw green mountains overlooking the beach, and God again reminded me how small I am compared to it all. I have almost zero balance but miraculously managed to not fall off the SUP board - one of my biggest achievements in recent years. And I had run a marathon the year before.

I remember how much energy I draw from being outside, and when confronted with God's majesty through nature. Paraty turned out to be another stop on the itinerary that blew our expectations out of the water. I walked the cobbled streets with Danielle that same day, holding her hand and squeezing it tightly as I realised the grace in that moment. A powerful impulse told me that nothing that God orchestrates could be broken, and we skipped our way past the colourful buildings of a town spoiled with immensely beautiful architecture.

A few days later we made the trip back to our original destination of Rio de Janeiro, and got on a minibus that had no suspension. My bum and my Garmin sport watch confirmed this as the bumpy ride helped me reach my daily "stairs goal" without me getting out of my seat for five hours. All of this didn't matter, as the kindness of the client liaison officer at our hotel in Jabaquara, the smile of the guy who made our melted cheese sandwiches, and the smell of roasted coffee from a plain-looking young lady reminded me how pretty life can be without my own ungrateful insecurities. By this stage I was thinking of buying some Speedos in bulk, as I kept letting go of the worldly nonsense deeply entrenched.

The week in Rio de Janeiro did not disappoint, and the dirt road of travelling abroad has by now been smoothed over by the metaphorical tar of rediscovery. At this stage it felt like smooth sailing, or rather speed boat cruising, with three precious weeks in Brazil coming to an end. We visited the iconic Christ De Redeemer statue, where I had another insight which told me that since moving closer to the feet of Jesus, my life had taken a turn for the better. It was a symbolic realisation expressed by a world-renowned statue of our Saviour. There is no better moment of rediscovery than the realisation that you are loved, and you have grace and an abundance of blessings in your life. It does not require travelling, but travelling accelerates the process and highlights its significance, without a doubt. The answer of who I really am doesn't reside in a world full of agendas but rather in the inner chambers of the heart. It was all hand-crafted and deposited in those chambers. Your treasures and favour are also waiting to be rediscovered. The reward is too great to not at least try.

As we walked the Copacabana Beach strip, I could not stop smiling. We popped in at a local restaurant for another delicious Brazilian meal. I discovered tapioca flour and acai bowls, which gave me enough reason for a few more fist pumps. On one of the last days before we returned home, we headed down to Ipanema Beach and I saw an area that looked good for swimming. Danielle agreed to look after the valuables and I rushed into the ocean with the same excitement a small child has when opening his gifts on Christmas. I tried to look competent but got thrown over by a few waves. I decided to call it quits and tried my utmost to walk out of the ocean like a member of the Baywatch cast. Still no Speedo. We slowly moved to a more reasonable spot with less intimidating waters. I swam there for more than an hour and thought of nothing.

We made our way back to the hotel and it was my turn to look after the beach towels and money bag. Danielle went into the water and pulled off the perfect Baywatch entry. I smiled and my heart swelled with pride. All of a sudden her arms started flapping like an injured bird and she was shouting at me in pure desperation. She was surrounded by two sea turtles. I saw their heads breaching the water.

Magically, Danielle got her moment with the sea turtles; she swam with them for probably thirty to forty minutes. Everyone got excited and the buzz on the beach was electric. We reluctantly went back to the hotel as the sun set over the iconic landmark. What a beautiful day. I felt at peace and appreciated the opportunity to rediscover, remembering who I am, what I enjoy, and where my identity lies. What is yours? Travelling will help you to rediscover these valuable truths.

The rediscovery which took place in Brazil was immeasurable and cannot be paid for by credit card. If you feel that your mind might be filled with too many unrelated thoughts, lies, false expectations and negativity, I beg you to consider a Monkey Lion adventure. You need to leave your comfort zone in order to obtain the precious gift of rediscovery. You learn to appreciate the small things again; you see how blessed you really are and how much God loves you. It makes you feel small and naturally makes your own world look smaller too. We get stuck in the "big fish living in a small pond" syndrome, where we think our own world is so big and important. It really is not that important at all. It is a microscopic molecule in the greater scheme of things. Someone needed to hear that today.

Brazil reminded me that I should stop chasing goals, financial gain, status, etc. It is just not me. It gave me a better understanding of the importance of being rested so you can achieve the only goal that really matters - being happy. Remember that God is in control, not us. We need to trust Him and stop trying to achieve contentment out of our own efforts. I would, in fact, recommend receiving contentment from Him. You have your own perspective that you need to rediscover or be reminded of. A wonderful way for you to access this is by taking a trip abroad or venturing on a road trip to the nearest wilderness in your proximity. Go out there and rediscover who you are and what you love! Even if that means going to a place that is all about soul searching and G-string bikinis.

THE MONKEY LION
ANALOGY

We have reached the final chapter of this book and I will finish off by reiterating the Monkey Lion analogy. This analogy emphasises how travelling provides you with the opportunity to excel personal growth. We need to stop over-thinking things out of fear and trust our instinct, much as a monkey would do, and live our lives with the bold bravery that is found in the heart of a lion. I urge you to write your own story through exploring the world. And if you have already started, do not stop.

There is no specific formula or structure for this process, and each of us has a different journey to undertake. During the process, everything happens on its own time, and patience is key. I know that travelling and exploring the globe has helped me with my story and my progress. Most importantly, in a very unexpected way, it has allowed me to reflect on where I have been in order to give me some indication of where I am going. My journey has been transformational and has allowed for personal growth through all the adventures mentioned in this book, and more.

It is not always possible to travel and we all have responsibilities, but I am asking, begging and encouraging you to prioritise adventure in your life. Do not just drive to the supermarket. Try walking to the shops for some bread, milk and ice cream, and do not forget to rally your spouse and the children. It is a mindset. Take hold of the so-called Monkey Lion analogy: do not overthink things, but step up and embrace an adventurous lifestyle. Pray about it and ask God to open the doors for you. He is the orchestrator of all things and will answer the prayers of the righteous. It is about access, not ownership; and opportunities are around every corner. Allow yourself to be creative and adventurous.

Make a list of the places you have always wanted to visit and start saving up for the adventures that will change your life. The reward of stepping out of your comfort zone is immeasurable. It works best when you are meeting new people and seeing new places. Make another list of adventures you can conquer locally and take some time to go and do them. Be brave and be bold. One of the best parts about travelling lies in the planning, and the better you plan, the more you will be able to discover. Also remember that it is not about spending on luxurious breakaways. In fact, I would recommend planning cheaper trips - they are my personal favourites. It does not necessarily have to cost you an arm and a leg.

Another suggestion would be to look next door and visit a neighbouring country. Some of the world's greatest gems might be right in front of you. We get fixated on far-off exotic destinations because they feature in our web search. You are going to have to think and act against the grain when embarking on this magical journey. People tend to say that it is better to go to college first, work hard and then travel when retired. I completely disagree. I believe that it should be done from a young age. This allows you to grow and experience as much of life as possible. If you are young and unsure of what you want to do with your life, please consider taking a gap year, or even two if need be. It might just steer you in an unexpected direction, straight towards the career or lifestyle you were always meant to have and enjoy. Remember that you will learn as you go, regardless of your age.

I would also encourage you to make notes of your adventures and take lots of photos. They will be critical for reflection, as I have discovered on this adventure of writing my first book. It's human nature to forget, and writing or journalling can serve as a handy reminder when memories start to become a bit vague or are even lost. It will put a smile on your face upon review. There is also the inevitable travel hangover to consider, and writing a short memoir after returning home helps to process the experience. Another awesome cure is to plan the next trip. It is hard to go back to normal upon returning home after one of these adventures.

I truly hope that this book and the abstract analogy of travelling like a Monkey Lion has inspired you to plan a trip, book a flight or dust off the hiking gear. I hope your travels will be filled with many magical moments and that you will grow through all your unique experiences. I hope you find lifelong friendships, enduring love, fiery passion, sharp humour, difficult challenges, warm smiles and God's presence while being a typical travelling Monkey Lion.

I hope that you will share your experiences with the travelling community. Let's keep encouraging one another to never stop travelling. So here's to never over-thinking things out of fear, but trusting our instincts, as monkeys might, and to living life with the bold bravery found in the hearts of lions. See you on the road.

Milton Keynes UK
Ingram Content Group UK Ltd.
UKHW011502170624
444324UK00038B/521

9 781922 803207